Talking Politics

Talking Politics:
The Substance of Style from Abe to "W"

Michael Silverstein

PRICKLY PARADIGM PRESS
CHICAGO

Prickly Paradigm Press, LLC
5629 South University Avenue
Chicago, Il 60637

www.prickly-paradigm.com

ISBN: 0-9717575-5-0
LCCN: 2002115993

Printed in the United States of America on acid-free
paper.

No doubt about it. Abraham Lincoln gets the prize among United States presidents for the sheer concentrated political power of his rhetoric. When he set his—actual, own—mind to preparing his text, he could come up with gems such as his Second Inaugural and, of course, his 272-word "Dedicatory Remarks" at Gettysburg. Even his extemporaneous public and private talk, transcribed, shows great verbal ability. Now Mr. Lincoln had no Yale or Harvard degree as a credential of his education. But he understood the aesthetic—the style, if you will—for summoning to his talk the deeply Christian yet rationalist aspirations of America's then four-score-and-seven-year-old polity. Striving to realize this complex style, he polished it and elaborated its contours. He embodied the style. So much so, that Lincoln's great later texts, like the late, great man himself, now belong to the ages. They form part of the liturgy of what Robert Bellah has termed America's "civil religion."

And Americans ever since have at least officially identified masterly political accomplishment with public stylistic communication in the shadow of Lincoln: FDR, JFK, and Ronald Reagan, for example, in the twentieth century. Each was memorable for initiation or mastery of a signature public communicative style. No matter what went on in private, no matter what the policy failings and scandals of their administrations, their genres of address developed this tradition of presidential style in certain ways. And presidential style, as opposed to other things, does "trickle down" to influence all the levels of politics and layers of American government.

By contrast, who can be comfortable with the notion that a "great" president would not also be a great communicator, especially when speechifying in person and on broadcast media? Political figures like this are puzzling; those who rate and rank former presidents have trouble deciding where to put them in the list. Observe the jitteriness that pop historians have about Eisenhower, whose best speech was probably his televised farewell address a couple of evenings before the Kennedy era. (He had had eight years to rehearse this grandfatherly valedictory.) Or Truman, with his reputation for schmoozy, street-smart vulgarity displayed right out in the open. And observe the revulsion that still counteracts what admiration people may feel about Richard Nixon's accomplishments, this president who in his public address style always seemed not quite successfully to be hiding something. These days his paranoid Oval Office ravings—replete with loads of *f*- and *n*-words!—circulate in public, transcribed from tapes slowly seeping out of an archival sewerful of I-told-you-so conversational sludge (the shit has hit his erstwhile fans, as it were!).

From Lincoln's Gettysburg, flash forward another seven score years. Like language itself, presidential communication styles do change. Here's George Walker Bush, a.k.a. "Dubya:"

> Natural gas is hemispheric. I like to call it hemispheric in nature because it is a product that we can find in our neighborhoods.

Dyslexic? Just stupid? Out of his league? *His* "League" is the Ivy one: this man has *both* Yale *and* Harvard degrees! (Want a refund, Poppy?) And, notwithstanding his actual installation as President in 2000 by a 5-4 vote in the U. S. Supreme Court, he did manage to garner a certified 47.9% of the popular vote, all throughout the heartland of America. By 2002, he even managed to develop wartime "presidential coattails" stumping to win a Republican Congress. He must be communicating *something* attractive to a large fraction of the electorate (besides merely "Being There" in 2000 as a non-Clintongore alternative). That something is clearly not Lincolnesque, however, much as our voting contemporaries seem to respond to his "message." And if certain folks have reacted with supercilious or nerdy disdain, not to say late-night comical guffaws and doctored jpegs on the net (see below), I maintain that the "W" style is fully *within* the culture of political communication the huffy critics and winking satirists intuitively understand and engage.

Rather than getting upset, we ought to pause, take an analytic view of the matter, and put this President's communicative performance into context. I think this will make understandable why he just might not be a mere aberration but a slight readjustment of the terms of politics the country has operated on all along! The current President, then, just might be the very cynosure of what now "sells," pointing in the direction as well of political communication to come. Goodbye Lincoln, hello Dubya! And after "W," the end of the alphabet of politics.

Communicating the Message vs. Inhabiting "Message"

The substance of it all, I would contend, is style. The technicians of political communication have their own term that gestures toward it: "message," as in "being on message" or "being off message" or "sticking to [no "the"] message." As an insider's technical term, "message" is moving from what we call a count noun, that denotes a specific individuable thing, to one that denotes a locus or place in a containing space, realm, or condition of being. (Think of the difference between <u>the</u> [telephone] <u>call</u> you made last evening and [being] <u>on</u> <u>call</u>.) "Message" is inhabitable: "*my* message" is like my house. That's key.

Those not attuned to politicoglossia may at first think that someone's "message" is the topic, or theme, or central proposition he or she is trying to communicate. You might identify it—in fact, the professionals hope reporters and others will *misidentify* it—with the "point" of an occurrence of communication. You could paraphrase someone's "point" as a kind of assertion that such-and-such is the case about something-or-other.

You would be wrong. Professionals want, in fact, to *suggest* this to you. (Frequently the professionals are just able to rely on the flat-footedness of print-media reporters; they were focused in journalism school on finding and paraphrasing actual statements in an "objective" manner, and so they continue to look for them.) But media professionals also want you to be wrong in your hasty attribution, because that will make it harder to figure out the trick to the magic: did he say so or didn't he? (Did he promise not to raise taxes or didn't he? What did he claim—or just lead us to believe—about "that woman?") "Message," we can discern from the study of political communication, is really much more complicated than that. If successful, a person comes to inhabit "message" in the act of communicating. And if "the people"—and their press corps—want to think that it is what someone actually said, that's *their* problem—and it's our politico's success at "messag[e]"ing. Let me explain, by way of describing the several ways we communicate using language.

One part of us intuitively feels that the language we use consists of the words and expressions we speak, write, or otherwise get across to our addressees along some channel of communication. We recognize ourselves to be sending and receiving such language forms. In order to understand "message," however, we have to think about the several different kinds of meaningfulness always present—though not always recognized—when language is used. We have to look at other principles that organize our communications to see what is central to "message." But let's start with words and phrases.

In our own intellectual tradition of understanding how people use language, the most salient—the *official*—"what" of communication lies in how words and expressions describe, or in technical terms, denote. We explicitly describe things by naming them in category [*Examples*: ...<u>table</u>...; ...<u>five</u>-<u>cent</u> <u>cigar</u>...;

etc.]. We implicate a description of things whenever we get agreement—or at least do not get disagreement—to a claim we've communicated about them that such-and-so is the case (or was the case, or might be the case, etc.). (The claim is frequently in relation to something else, already described or presumed to be known.) [*Examples:* (Your horse's name here)...<u>would</u> <u>have</u> <u>been</u> <u>running</u> <u>at</u> <u>The</u> <u>Preakness</u> <u>next</u> <u>week</u>; (Your name here)...<u>will</u> <u>not</u> <u>have</u> <u>a</u> <u>hard</u> <u>time</u> <u>understanding</u> <u>this</u>; etc.]. Understanding each other in communication is really coming to sufficiently common focus on what these descriptions, explicit and implicated, are and apply to.

So *officially* we describe things and states-of-affairs so that others can also identify those things and states-of-affairs. The official message is the complex, identifying description—the *information structure*—we achieve over the longer haul of paragraphs and whole disquisition-sized chunks of verbiage by using words and expressions linked one to another by grammatical and other rules.

Of course we have to know certain grammatical rules of sentence-formation. That, for example, in English descriptions at least, an expression that explicitly describes a thing (<u>John</u>...) precedes an implicated descriptive expression for it (...<u>went</u> <u>to</u> <u>the</u> <u>store</u>.). We know a myriad of such grammatical rules relating to the structure of sentences, phrases, and the like.

But additionally, there are principles based in developing information-structure itself, distinct from the grammar of sentences, that determine what expressions we can and do use at various points in communication. As everyone knows, while communication proceeds, sender and receiver can rely more and more on what has already been communicated about a topic, information about it that cumulates between them. Based on this growing intersubjective pool of information, fluently deployed descriptions of the very same thing can differ in form, depending on where in a text they occur. What earlier in discourse-time one may have described as "a large, brown bear" one describes, a bit later as "it" or "the beast" or even "the thing I was just writing about"—the large brown bear I focused you on, that is, even in the absence of an actual critter to point to! However unconsciously, a careful talker monitors the flow of text-in-progress, if only at the level of knowing that he or she is making not only grammatical sense on a sentence-by-sentence basis, but also informational sense over the longer haul. Demanding addressees expect no less of our information-packaging.

In this way, discourse is always being evaluated as description for how it achieves a kind of cumulative coherence as information. Under the umbrella of this kind of meaningfulness, people can actually *inform* one another about the things and states-of-affairs they communicate about. Our talk can cause others to reach, with us, an intersubjective identification of things. And not just identification, but identification *as categorized* according to our particular descriptive language at a particular moment in discourse. We can successfully use language to inform others even if our interlocutors had previously had some other ideas about these very matters. We can even *mutually inform* one another, each interlocutory partner contributing some bit of information to the emerging whole. Whether in a single instance of communication or over a chain of instances, then, people can use language to construct collectively reached and collectively consequential knowledge, opinion, and belief about all manner of things. In principle descriptive language can be fashioned into a tool or instrument for constructing sharable knowledge in the very event of communication.

But, having mentioned both grammar and information structure, is there anything else to communicative use of words and expressions? Are there other factors that explain why we use one expression rather than another at any given momentary phase of communication? For example, why do we characteristically use one word or expression that might describe something and altogether avoid another one that would, in principle, be equally descriptive? (Did he say "the *Democratic* proposal"—or was it "*democratic*?"—or did he call it a "*Democrat*" one?) It turns out that in every discourse a large number of extra-verbal contextual factors leave their determinate traces in the forms we use—what are termed in the trade *indexical* (pointing) traces. These traces inform us about, they point to, the who-what-where-when-why of discourse by subtle loadings of the "how," the actual forms, of discourse. ("Democratic" or "Democrat?" Republican Party operatives these days teach their politicians to avoid the first, older and official name that ends with "-ic" and to use the second form, without it. For political partisans, remember, there is real danger that the

"-ic" form would simultaneously convey the meaning of the lower-case d-word, <u>democratic</u>, as what those other guys are about! So adhering to this rule while speaking self-identifies the very speaker of the form as being in one political party category rather than the other.) Indexical values of language forms locate and identify the parties to the communication where they are used the way a good pantomime gives the impression of taking place in a comprehensible surround.

These indexical factors in language seem to crosscut the information structure always emerging via grammar and denotational coherence as speakers add to the words and expressions in a text. Masters of political "message," just like other users of languages, have intuitively known all along about the indexical power of the words they use, and especially about the cumulative indexical poetry of properly arranged words. Such masters have had a knack for indexical design that has shaped each era's political communication—at least as much as the descriptive content of it (if any)—thus creating a true rhetorician's art form. Even the great "message" master, Lincoln.

In this way the actual forms of language in use concretize both the momentary and the more enduring arrangements of us people engaged in communicating, the ways we arrange ourselves in space-time and categorize each other in social life. And doubly so. In communicating we certainly *rely* on social arrangements already in place, and the expectations we can then have about what form talk should take between two socially locatable individuals. But as well, each time we deploy specific forms of language we *create* social arrangements as consequences of using these forms; we bring new social arrangements into being. In the most smoothly executed cases, all parties just implicitly understand and act upon the consequentialities of how we communicate—sometimes even in ways that violate normative expectation.

When we are brought together by communication we depend on the fact that we are always already socially arranged one with respect to another in an intuitive sociocultural categorization. All of us are identifiable as being of one or another kind, to one or another degree, both enduringly and momentarily. Even to get communication started with others depends on making certain assumptions about whom—i.e., what kind of person—we're communicating with. (Think of identities constructed and imagined on the internet.) We expect certain kinds of communicative forms to emerge, certain kinds of uses of language and such. But—importantly—the act of communication itself, that is, the emergence of certain indexically potent message forms, can always transform the intuitive classifications we apply to one another, new ones suddenly pointed to as now operative and consequential for an interaction.

What indicative signs or signals, for example, were you relying on in your aunt's talk when you concluded, the other day, that she was "stressed?" After all, she didn't describe herself that way by actually saying something like "I'm working under a lot of stress these days!" or "I feel under a lot of pressure." Yet you gave her uncharacteristic latitude in your conversation. Again, how did I come to know that the prospective student in my office last week was gay? He did not announce this to me as a self-description, explicit or implicit. He just talked about—*described*, in the sense I discussed earlier—why he was interested in a particular educational degree program. These kinds of inferential processes go on constantly in interaction, as we all know, on the basis of indexical signals that work like gestures in pantomime.

In essence we continuously point to our own—and, relationally, then, to our interlocutor's—transient and more enduring identities. Interactions as events develop these relational identities as consequences of communicative behavior. The clarity of identities comes in phases, punctuated by shifts over interactional time: what-you-and-I-*are* in a moment of interaction strives to become what-you-and-I-*will-be*. We effortlessly factor all this in to the conversational import and impact of talk we engage in, just as we try to do so for talk we observe and analyze as social scientists or students of rhetoric, or for talk we create and represent as novelists or playwrights. We have always operated with these effects as unremarkable but essential truisms of talk, yet linguists have only recently brought them into sharp and analytic view. Why?

These demonstrations of and inferences about identities are very much the usual and "other" business of communication. Yet they have been largely out of the aware consciousness of communicators, for two related reasons. One is that the most obvious signals of inhabitable identity seem to be un-language-like, even though in actual communication they are jumbled together with what we recognize as the descriptive structuring of language. A recurrent sighing timbre of the voice. (Do we have a special sign in the way we would write this down?) A particular pronunciation pattern of certain consonants and vowels. (All we write with an alphabet is a sign for the identity of the consonant or vowel.) So we tend not to recognize these as central to communication—until, perhaps, they are removed, as in much early computer-generated robotic speech, and we realize that the message we're hearing no longer sounds human!

Second, all of the institutionalized technologies of language have cumulatively reinforced this intuitive difficulty of explicit recognition by concentrating on its descriptive functions. Grudgingly, the other stuff may be "added on"—as "art!" By institutionalized technologies I mean everything from the writing and printing conventions to the personnel and paraphernalia of enforcing standard languages: dictionaries, thesauruses, grammars, manuals of style, and the people who create them and insist that they are authoritative. Such official biases about language have a kind of feedback effect on how we view what is the "real" language and what is unimportant or peripheral—good for art, perhaps, as it tries to imitate life, but hardly the stuff of life's serious communication! The biases, built into our institutional forms across the board, keep telling us to discount what is actually indispensable to normal and effective human communication.

Indeed, official views of communication center on "book larnin'" (as it is ridiculed). They hyper-

emphasize the use of language for descriptive purposes, sometimes foolishly and vainly attempting to
disregard the inevitable, simultaneous use of language
for inhabiting identities. And, of course, just such ways
of fashioning inhabitable identities in communication
give our messages whatever life-like appeal they may
have.

There are many ways we go about indexically
defining relevant identities. The register of language
we use, in respect of words, phrases, sentence length
and range of grammatical structures. (Did we "empty
the container of its contents" or "get the stuff out?")
The fluency and sheer amount of language we use in a
turn of communication. The paragraph-sized structures of coherence we build up over time, like rhythms
of other bodily action. In spoken language, our "tone
of voice," as people term a range of things from stress
and intonation patterns that depend on phraseology,
all the way to characteristic pitch range, melodious-
ness and other dynamic qualities of phonation.
Gesture, movement and stasis of body regions,
dynamic face-work, etc., micro-synchronized, as we
have discovered from film and videotape analysis, with
the flow of descriptive language forms. Gestural
actions performed while communicating verbally, or,
sometimes equivalently, simply by communicating
nonverbally—like making the Sign of the Cross with
or without a simultaneous blessing of someone or
something. A careful student of communication wants
to record all of these kinds of things, laboriously and
in detail. They constitute the additional material along
with which purely descriptive language flows among

interlocutors. Carefully analyzing this, we can get an idea of the ways that identities are being drawn upon and fashioned without ever being explicitly described.

Over multiple indexical channels, then, there comes into being a kind of poetry of identities-in-motion as the flow of communicative forms projects around the participants complex patterns—let's say "images"—not onto Plato's cave wall, but onto the potentially inhabitable and then actually inhabited context. So there is image. There is style. There is "message." Image is not necessarily visual; it is an abstract portrait of identity fashioned out of cumulating patterns of congruence across all manner of indexical signs—including visual ones—that addressees and audiences can imaginatively experience, like a hologram. Style—the way image is communicated—has degree and depth of organization; it may be consistent within an event, or over a series of them, or even across a whole biography. Whole institutions come to be embodied in particular communicative styles. (Remember *The Man in the Grey Flannel Suit*? Remember the late Dave Thomas of Wendy's Restaurants?) "Message," then, strategically deploys style to create image in a consequential way. "Message" stylists want good (that is, effective) ones to be cumulative and lasting among a target set of addressees. They see "message" as potentially enhancing somebody's chances in a "market" that validates that somebody's worth in a desired and expectable way. "Message" projects out from the communicational here-and-now we're experiencing as it is being created. It seeks to connect us with someone's desired futurities in which we and they will play a role.

So being "on message" contributes to that consistent, cumulative, and consequential image that a public person has among his or her addressed audience. A really powerful "message" ascribes to me—as opposed to describes—my reality. It allows my audience to image-ine a whole set of plausible stories in the fictive universes of the must-have-been, the could-be, and, especially, the sure-as-hell-will-be ("I'll vote for *that*!"). Votes are such stuff as dreams are made on—and vice versa.

The Dream Machine is a Magnet for "Issues"

"Debate the issues! Debate the issues!" some people constantly scream along with the print press—cold type no doubt fancying itself the embodiment of steely reason in the media age. Are these cries for "issues" reaching the stubbornly deaf ears of the indifferent (i.e., leading or successful) pols and their media mavens? Issues are supposed to be the thing, no? Not just a ploy laid on by an invisible, "message"-less loser? Sure, they are vital matters in which we severally have stakes, that we can rationally focus upon by the use of expository communication, language that lays them out in some denotationally orderly way for deliberative decision-making—right? Right?

In today's politics, just as—it turns out—in past political life, expository communication can play as large or as little a stylistic role as is required by the image one's "message" needs to create. At one extreme, fringe candidates of both the left and the right seem to rely too much on civics-book imagery of The League of Women Voters (no gender affront intended!). And not only because they are generally losers in the political process. Taking such manuals with a bloodless literalism, they always rely on discussion of—as they are called in politics—"the issues." Minutely laying out their positions, they treat the voters to displays of long-winded disquisitions and debater's points. They insist on retracing all the steps of the argument—especially for the convinced faithful, who get a recharging buzz out of this old-time, from-first-principles liturgy. And they hope to appeal as well to whoever will listen among outsiders to the faith, evangelizing them. It can be a Naderesque (or Chomskian!) argument against documented influence of big corporate interests, inexorably moving from statistics to interpretative hypothesis to hortatory platform plank. Or it can be an Alan Keyes finding Scriptural bases and other truly first principles to challenge our merely practical patchwork of case-based legal precedents on abortion—on which he will also demand that other candidates be equally clear and decisive.

In both cases, the "message" being conveyed is, in actuality, the speaker's rigidity, narrowness, and myopia. What gets conveyed is a noncompromisable, theory-driven perspective on the world. Its positions on "the" issues have clear implications for what— purely rationally within that worldview—to do and not to do. In today's politics, certainly, such issue-consumed figures can easily be seen as lacking "message" entirely, or at least confusing it with the actual set of "issues" they endlessly discourse about. When the public searches for "message" with these folks—as it inevitably must, say I—the best it can do is to use the label "single-issue candidate," discerning perhaps some one generalized issue through the interpretative lens of "message," no matter how many actual substantive "issues" the candidate may have attempted to bring up and address.

That is not to say that "message" cannot be built around "issues"; it always is, or at least must be made to seem so. Just not usually around the kind of

issues that have that first-principles, wordy-disquisi-
tional ring to them. For example, Mr. Clinton's more-
or-less admitted philandering was an "issue" in the
2000 presidential elections. Republican interests had
long since defined his "bimbo eruptions" in the
Arkansas Democrat[ic] tradition of Governor
Winthrop Rockefeller and Representative Wilbur
Mills for "message"-relevance. They were offenses
against traditional marriage (not, for example, matters
of abuse of power crossing gender relations, a left-lib-
eral—as in "Hey! *Their* guy!"—issue). It was all but
declared that that "Women's Libber"—now Senator—
Hillary Rodham Clinton seemed somehow to deserve
her errant husband's behavior. So Republicans theatri-
cally professed moral outrage to all media who would
listen—as they whispered all the rumored names and
dates to all available Special Prosecutors.

It is not surprising then that in the 2000 election the Democratic presidential candidate sought to
emphasize the self-distancing, countervailing "message" demanded as much by his own side as by the
other one. To be sure, when repeatedly asked point
blank about the matter, assuming the allegations were
all true, Mr. Gore, then the sitting Vice-President to
Mr. Clinton, had to cast clear, if gentle, aspersions on
the President's morality. But that's merely a somewhat
quote-worthy one-liner of judgmental discourse. By
contrast, who in the television audience of the
Democratic Convention can forget Mr. Gore's "sur-
prise" appearance, violating the tradition of the nomi-
nee's seclusion, as he went rushing to the podium to
give his own actual wife a long, passionate—marital!—

kiss after she gave a speech? A moment, clearly, to be "on message" in relation to an unspoken (as well as both unspeakable and unmentionable!) "issue."

Floridly and publicly inhabiting such—as we might term it—zipped fidelity fits into a larger set of "message"-worthy issues that Mr. Gore and his campaign were clearly sensitive to as they sought routes to his own "message" of fundamental personal distinctness, if not radical policy difference, from Mr. Clinton. Republicans, of course, have more generally been mercilessly beating Democrats with issues of this kind since the 1960s, as the newly Republican Sunbelt and the Christian right-wing became focal to their electoral strategy. They have been lump-summed as captioned "social issues" for strategic purposes of "message" appeal (and for a systematic and large-scale diversionary conspiracy—while S&L's, Enron, and WorldCom burn—especially to keep the traditionally Democratic political left permanently occupied in federal court, burdened with huge legal expenses to litigate before increasingly Republican-appointed federal judges). Indeed, to the contemporary Pat-and-Rush segment of the politically aware, Bill Clinton's moral offenses, as "message"-relevant, were part of a package of issue-emblems, standing for everything bad from equity feminism, *Roe v. Wade*, and gay liberation, to lack of compulsory school prayer, "government intervention" by banning (guns) and planning (economies), "socialized medicine" (a 1950s AMA expression brought out of mothballs by a desperate George H. W. Bush during the 1992 election campaign!) and thence—of course—to Communism (now perhaps Islam).

But how does one get from one of these issues to the next, so that by this form of associative stepping from stone to stone, the lot of 'em can be seen to form an available pool of targetable "issues?" If this can be achieved, then any one of them, deployed on some occasion, summons up the rest, and—read through the totality—projects into inhabitable image? How does what impresses us as the very height of *illogic* have a processual "logic" of its own, such that successful politicians' discourse respects this logic? And where can we see these processes at work, where "issues" get lumped and turned into "message"-operators available for stylistic fashioning of image? How does a politician fashion "message" as a kind of magnet for sometimes randomly assembled "issues," that clump to it like iron filings arrayed in its magnetic field?

Interestingly, there is in this something of what the great "Russian" (i.e., Soviet and Jewish) psychologist Lev Vygotskij termed "thinking in complexes." A complex, Vygotskij maintained, differs from a full rational or scientific concept, though both are discernible in psychological processes of grouping things, of classifying them as "the same," or as instances of some principle of "equivalence." We might be able to lay out a series of things lumped together via thinking-in-complexes so that, taken two-by-two, each pair of them will show at least a local "family resemblance" in some respects, but the whole lot of things might still be very diverse overall, especially so for things at distant remove in the process. (Of course, this is what we find in nature with members of what are termed "species" in appearance, physiology, and life-course, the biologists' "phenotype" characteristics. And certainly with any examples of social and cultural phenomena.)

Psychologically, then, "complex"-thinking is a conceptual process that results in classifying things together that may be related one to another by analogies and other kinds of term-by-term similarity. But after the fact, we are sometimes hard-pressed to extract what holds this complex together, except that we have created it by jumping from one thing to the next. Do you know that game where you start with a spelled-out word and then change one letter at a time until you have transformed the original into a word that makes a striking meaning contrast with the first one? S-I-T > S-I-N > S-U-N > R-U-N. Taken in pairs, the terms in the game looks very, very similar, yet the ones at the two ends of the chain are very, very different. Vygotskij thought that children go through more and more stable and encompassing forms of thinking in complexes, readying the developing mind for true conceptual use of language. He observed that even for us thinking adults, most of the expressions of our private, fantasy discourses have chain-complex meanings, rather than fully conceptual ones—as does a great deal of our own and others' everyday use of language.

Indeed, listen to someone thinking out loud in complexes, sometimes even about very serious matters, rather than in scientific (i.e., fully rational) conceptual terms. One hears, step by step, the way that in the narrative a particular point begins to morph with rhetorical liquidity into the plot of another narrative, and so on, sometimes over very large stretches of talk. At each such jump, the characters and things and situations are, willy-nilly, lined up in a kind of direct or inverse parallel—a kind of equivalence—to those of the previous segment of discourse. Trading experiences informally with others, we all engage in this all the time, the cohesive principle over which is the likeness or structured transformation-of-likeness from one segment to another. "Shooting the breeze" or whatever one calls it when we dive into conversation with "That reminds me of…:" the exemplary people, things, and situations of such wandering narratives implicitly grow as chained analogues. Such thought-about but unfocused narrative relations, if seized upon by a pregnant captioning label or image, suddenly make the whole analogical series take on a definitive identity—in fact retrospectively a *necessary* identity that we now recognize as so many examples of one underlying principle, conceptually implicit, even immanent. "So *that's* what it is!"

Even the Anglo-American case-law tradition operates this way, as the late Attorney-General Edward H. Levi long ago noted. The "finding" of precedent—as though discovering a set of further instances of a scientific covering law—for concluding a case under adjudication is the name of the game. It requires that a brief or a decision create a "deductive" argument about analogues across a (historical) chain of other, already settled cases that, one claims, are to be united under a single principle, the one that must be applied to this case, here and now—a principle which, at the so-called growth edges of law, may have never before been explicitly known and labeled as such, note! So chain-complex gives birth to concept. (Given the case-by-case way our legal process operates, it's no wonder lawyers on political missions itch to get the proverbial foot-in-the-door case on issues like restricting abortion, or search and seizure, or rights to firearms, in order to begin establishing an analogic chain complex in which conceptually rationalizable "precedent" can be discovered.)

In politics, likewise, it's chain complexes of "issues" all the way down. Issues are the raw semiotic material, the things-in-reality. To give birth to "message" issues must be brought together—given plot and characters, rhyme if not reason—in occasions devoted to the making of image. The best occasions of this sort combine the use of verbal discourse situated in the context of a reinforcing sound-and-light show. In good political spectacle, whether experienced or merely imagined, the verbiage and other recognizable cultural symbols have to resonate one with another. A political figure needs to communicate—or to have been understood to communicate—the analogic "identity," the equivalence, of issues that go into "message" by fashioning organized, potent displays of them. The analogic bridge is critical, regardless of whether or not a linguistic communication "makes sense," scientifically or "conceptually"—though, as we'll see, until recently a fault of this sort was considered embarrassing. Success comes to him or her who can be positioned to embody the very essence, the principle, the "right stuff" that holds these issues together—"me."

Ah! To turn the chance of mere occasion into the necessity of my—of our—destiny! (Hence we can understand Mr. Gore's attempt to become a magnetic "message" for issues of inspiringly, refreshingly clean living in high places with his stylized impetuous kiss of "still-hot-to-trot-with-you-dear" middle-aged marital fidelity.) Success at this has been, is, and will continue to be the genius of the electorally successful in our kind of politics. That is the challenge to the fringe kooks who would "issue" us to death ("Hey! You're not talking about the [*my*] issues!") without ever getting to "message." Their "message" is the invidious one pinned on them by others like the proverbial tail on the donkey (even a non-Democratic one!), in stark contrast to their "message"-savvy opponents.

Let's see how "message" emerges at the two extremes of our political alphabet thus far: Abe and "W."

The Dash to "Message" in the Age of Telegraphy

Of course in the 1860s the media cycles so essential to "message" worked at a slightly slower pace than ours. No remote-location videocamera broadcasting. Events (even stenographic transcripts of speeches) could be reported to headquarters via telegraphy, and then circulated by newspapers and magazines and such. Editorially shaped, they circulated by print dissemination of news and opinion about them. Lithographic images of events and personalities, broadsides, and cartoons and caricatures were an essential part of mass print media. (Cartoons really came into their own, in fact, in the 1860 and especially 1864 campaigns.) Adjusting for this, we can learn much about the enduring substance of style from how Mr. Lincoln's only fitfully successful "message" got a new birth at Gettysburg—and defined him just in time for the impending ("North"-only) 1864 presidential election cycle!

It was no big deal that Mr. Lincoln—a savvy politician from frontier beginning to martyred end—did, in fact, shift in the weight he accorded to specific "issues" over the course of his political career. Circumstances demanded no less. The biggest issue was, of course, slavery, which had been driving apart the sectional interests of the country for several decades. (It was the elephant in the Republican Party's tent.) By dominating political parties, sectional interests competed to capture for themselves the newer

Plains and Prairie territories opening up to Euro-American settlement. How to Americanize and domesticate the frontier became one of the fronts for the slavery issue. Year after year, a series of Congressional tugs-of-war cycled around it. These struggles strained the very fibers binding the country together. Religiously inspired, evangelical moralists whipped up sentiment for abolition of slavery on the one side, even as their equally pious counterparts on the other side scripturally affirmed the justness of per-petuating it.

In his own political self-alignment, first Whig and then Republican, Lincoln came out clearly against slavery, but stopped far short of the religious fervor of those on the Abolitionist extreme. As a rising Illinois politician in mid-century, he became very visible on the national stage by his 1858 senatorial run against Stephen A. Douglas. Publicly, Lincoln fashioned his pro-Union arguments in the more strictly Constitutionalist terms that would see and call the Democratic Party's—and especially Douglas'—poker-game legislative tactics over the new territories. He advanced these issues as fronts for the *sl*-word (utter-ing which too clearly in the 1858 Illinois race against Stephen Douglas—and perhaps sounding too much like the Abolitionist extremists—may well have been a factor in Lincoln's loss). Lincoln was clearly on record as what we would term today a "white supremacist"; nonetheless, he committed himself at minimum to contain slavery territorially as an embarrassment of long standing, and certainly to sanitize the new Western territories from it. Ultimately, he argued, this would attenuate its economic grip everywhere and thus, in the end, serve the Union to be rid of it.

The crisis deepened, of course. The various political maneuvers hardened the determination of the two great sectional interests. One side formed the Northern and Midwestern manufacturing economy, wage-labor-based, with its agricultural and extractive hinterlands. The other side was the Southern agrarian plantocracy, plantation-centered and based heavily on racially marked slave labor and various forms of indenture.

After all the decades of thrust and parry in the skirmishes over slavery, at issue ultimately for Lincoln were the sacred and, for him, transcendent and irrevocable Union and its national constitutional processes. To what degree could the several states and territories go their separate ways with respect to property rights, rights of seizure, and rights of legal nullification and even secession? In a noticeably sectional election in November 1860 Lincoln became, in effect, the Northern and Pacific Coast President. (He got 2.48% of the votes in Maryland, 1.13% in Virginia, and 0.93% in Kentucky, for example, and otherwise none south of the Ohio River.) So, however lawyerly were his Daniel Webster-like arguments for maintaining the Union in response to the crisis—reviewed ever so carefully in his first Inaugural Address on 4 March 1861—by the time he was sworn into office the course had been prepared for descent into civil war with the secessionist Confederacy.

Only with hostilities under way do his highly public communications recognize that the Civil War was *de facto* about two regionally based economic systems, one of them based on slave labor and therefore repugnant to the idea of America that Jefferson's Declaration had argued in 1776 and that Madison's Constitution had formed into "a more perfect union" in 1787. This has certainly become central to Lincoln's most enduring "message."

Of course, he eventually acknowledged the Abolitionists' moral argument that condemned slavery altogether. He even embraced it *de jure*—viz., the Emancipation Proclamation announced in late 1862 and other measures. Lincoln was reelected in 1864 as a Union victory was just a matter of time, and his second Inaugural Address of 4 March 1865, a month before his Good Friday assassination, is a pietistic preachment on this theme of slave labor, strategically downplaying the sectionalism of moral indignation. With profound, biblical phrasing Lincoln sees slavery and its resulting war as a plague visited on all of American humanity by a classic Old Testament God. He concluded with his humble Christian call for his countrymen's "malice toward none" and "charity for all" in "achiev[ing] and cherish[ing] a just and lasting peace, among ourselves, and with all nations." Amen. A prayer come straight out of the liturgy!

In such a turn of phrase, we glimpse one of the hallmarks of Lincoln's "message." It was consistent all during his rise to political prominence, even though it became more majestically embellished and most widely appreciated only in his martyrdom: he was, Christ-like (assassinated on Good Friday!), the very embodied recapitulation of the narrative—the word made flesh—of American civic morality. "Out of the very earth, unancestried, unprivileged, unknown," as Boston Brahmin James Russell Lowell had termed him, Lincoln the autodidact frontiersman had matured into the plain-speaking, practical Evangelical Christian preacher of and for this special nation's indissoluble, transcendent moral unity "under God." He, the natural Everyman of American soil, was ultimately to save America from itself—that is, from the wicked, unjust ways into which at least some of the brethren had fallen—through his own determined self-sacrifice.

For many people, then, Lincoln embodied in his life—as he does more universally in the everlasting civic life that is his death—the true American voice. It is a voice that, in his turn, Carl Sandburg was both to characterize and to recapture for a later generation: a sacred voice of civic plain-spokenness, inspired with Christian reason and able to articulate with conviction what is right and what is wrong in the world around it. Plainness, that anti-high-church virtue of so much of American Evangelical Protestantism, means also not being carried away by pomp of occasion or of high office in institutions of power. In our civic life, later generations have revered Lincoln for these embodied qualities, as they have also liked Harry Truman and Ronald Reagan for the same reason (whatever trouble they have had with "Give-'em-Hell" Harry's style of its expression).

The downside of this "message," at least for the rational elites, is the kind of anti-intellectualism that Richard Hofstadter traces to the Great

Awakenings and the mid-nineteenth century Evangelical denominationalisms. The sometimes fiery preacherly talk associated with them led ordinary people into irrationality: merely "feeling" God's presence in exuberant manifestations. But this provides to many a template for the effervescence of participation in the civil religion to which Lincoln at his "message" best still calls us. A mystical patriotism of feeling, called forth in spectacle by virtuoso deployment of verbal and other presentational styles.

Lincoln's actual physical voice was not an orator's; it was apparently somewhat thin, reedy, and relatively high-pitched. He was, if not actually uncomfortable in extemporaneous speaking, not at what he thought to be his best on such occasions. As President, he demurred from a great many such requests—even on the evening before the Gettysburg triumph—preferring to read aloud from his carefully composed and reworked written texts or even having them read out for him. And after a speech was delivered, he closely managed its editing and transmission in print. In his younger days he was known to hover over telegraph and newspaper desks whence emanated the texts to be circulated to his public.

It is clear that Lincoln was something of an intellectual, if only self-taught in the craft aspects of the gentlemanly arts of the well-bred still easily mistaken for deep thought. Even so he managed to constitute a "message" of the quintessential American—the forthrightly plain spoken rail-splitter, honest and direct; this voice speaks with a knowledge of the sacred texts of both Christian and civil religion. He came to inhabit this "message" of America that he himself, along with the press, was able to fashion.

When spoken, Lincoln's best prose was the oral poetry of plain style. As "message" its style resonated with ministerial and liturgical language even more than with the famous declamations of Daniel Webster, Henry Clay and other orators that Lincoln, among many, studied. The style was the currency of all the quintessentially American Protestant sects and denominations making up the very voting publics in the northern and border states. Wishfully projecting, contemporaries marveled at how Lincoln spoke in simple prose—like Shakespeare, it was said, and like God's Word in the King James and later, even plainer English-language Bibles. These texts are the emblems of enduring "Englishness" of culture that the minimally educated would know of, even if they did not know them. Lincoln was appreciated for composing his texts with what people identified as "Anglo-Saxon" words, rather than in complicated, Greco-Latinate words and phrases. Many people of the time were already jittery about immigrants and newly acquired Western populations, let alone about African Americans. Lincoln's "message" to them must have been a soothing racial balm, it is clear, as much as he himself carefully addressed the time-bomb issue of race. In crisis, the simpler "Anglo-Saxon" heritage of America, welling up from a mythic era even before the country's founding moment, rescues—preserves, sustains, gives new birth to—the nation. Under God.

Death and Life at Gettysburg

And of all of the sacred Lincolniana, The Gettysburg Address, once memorized by generations of elementary school children, has become the most hallowed text in America's civil religious canon. It epitomizes the voice of Lincoln, and hence the voice of America itself. It was a peak moment of Lincoln's "message," crafted to be such, a kind of apotheosis of his political life for which he has been evermore remembered. Professional scholars of rhetoric may revere his second Inaugural; us plain folks have internalized The Gettysburg Address. As it alludes to and quotes the Declaration of Independence, so even the Pledge of Allegiance was altered in turn to quote it ("…[one] nation, under God…"); and the three now constitute a recitational triad, an integral series of great moments of the people's rhetoric.

Why? Let's look at this text, and at the very occasion of its first delivery, the dedication ceremony of the national cemetery on the site of the famous battle. In retrospect, myths have grown up around both text and occasion that reveal why this was a magical moment in political "message"ing. The Gettysburg Address has become what we might call a "eucharistic" text of American identity. In the Eucharist of a Christian church service, our symbolic incorporation (eating and drinking) of Christ's transubstantiated "Body and Blood" ritually results, contrariwise, in our *being* incorporated *into* His body and blood made corporate on earth, the fellowship and institution of the church. (Lincoln actually plays upon this Eucharistic *chiasmus*, the figure of the cross, as upon Christ's—and all Christian, let alone Hellenic—martyrdom, in his speech.) Similarly, for generations Americans have re-read and re-cited The Gettysburg Address like a creed; in this, we reaffirm and transformatively renew and enhance our own incorporation into the American nation-state.

It is almost embarrassing to speak of this 270-odd-word text as an "address," though Lincoln did, indeed, "address" his audience at that sad place on 19 November 1863. It was only a little over four months since the Battle of Gettysburg had concluded on the 3rd of July that year. (Note: it was a series of attacks by the Confederate forces that the Union had repulsed just in time for the 4th of July, whose sacred text is— the Declaration of Independence!). The principal orator of the day was Edward Everett—Senator, Ambassador, Harvard president; Ralph Waldo Emerson's role-model—whose spellbinding, classically Hellenic funeral oration of two-plus hours the world has little noted nor long remembered. (Everett, the main act, took the lead in printing his oration as a pamphlet in early 1864, with the President's remarks as part of the additional material. The Everett text is accessibly reprinted as Appendix III.A. in Garry Wills' 1992 best-seller, *Lincoln at Gettysburg* [Simon & Schuster].)

By contrast, the President's "dedicatory remarks" (as the program listed Lincoln's address) constitutes a ritual poem so perfectly "on message"— even beyond the ritual space in which it was recited—

that once the larger public could read the transcript in the next-day's newspapers, it began to steal Everett's thunder. (How ironic, too! This was for a second time: in his oration Everett declared that he himself had been misguided in a politics of appeasement before the 1860 election—having run against Lincoln as the Vice-Presidential candidate of the Constitutional-Union Party, the party advocating any compromise whatsoever to get the Rebels back from the brink!)

But Lincoln knew a "message" opportunity when it presented itself. He had sought to be present at the solemn gathering, since he understood more than anyone how mired he was in political controversies relating to the first foundering, then merely stumbling Union military campaign, to his having suspended *habeas corpus*, to the unfair and unpopular military draft, to widespread war profiteering, and to a runaway economy, among other difficulties. General Meade's 4th of July non-loss at Gettysburg, and close upon it General Grant's brilliant success at Vicksburg, were, by contrast, important to re-emphasize in late 1863. There was a blistering firestorm of criticism in the opposition and foreign press, "Honest Abe," "Uncle Abe," "Father Abraham" images notwithstanding on the part of loyal media. Lincoln sensed how precariously perched he was in relation to the upcoming 1864 elections in which one of his former commanding generals, George McClellan, was already sure to be the Democratic candidate, and his own cabinet member, Salmon P. Chase of Treasury, was vigorously angling—only one among many—to supplant him as the Republican one. (Neither appeared at

Gettysburg, though both had been invited by the sponsoring multi-state "Board of Commissioners for the Soldiers' National Cemetery at Gettysburg.")

The cemetery dedication was shaping up as a very Republican event, orchestrated by the prominent Republican head Commissioner, Judge David Wills of Gettysburg, in a state of a very loyal Republican Governor, Andrew G. Curtin. In fact, sensing that this was the equivalent of what today we term a "photo op" in front of a friendly audience, some of the press criticized it as nothing more than a campaign show, "Patriotic Gore," indeed! Still, only a rather offhand invitation came to Lincoln at the beginning of November: asking him, as Chief Executive, to make "a few appropriate remarks" after the main funeral oration. (For this, to draw a crowd they had first secured the services of Everett, whose busy schedule—not Lincoln's—set the actual date). Even to secure the invitation for Lincoln, the Illinois Commissioner, Clark E. Carr, had to argue against widely shared doubts about "his ability to speak upon such a grave and solemn occasion as that of the memorial services." That Lincoln used the solemn ritual occasion to advantage for his "message" is, of course, an understatement. Even the viciously critical among the press, in dismissing it, understood in their negativity that it solidified the terms of Lincoln's political persona— what we would call his "message."

Now any ritual occasion—not only a cemetery dedication—is one that participants feel is transformative. It envelops people in a bounded spacetime where something "magical" happens, with effects lasting beyond that time and place. Think of the "text" of a ritual like a wedding—the sum total of what is said by participants, what is played, danced, sung, how it is all moved through space-and-time, displayed, etc. The text gets its transformative effectiveness or "oomph" as a function of a dense, internal arrangement of meaningful symbols as they are experienced together and refract off one another. Ritual texts project an air of self-sufficiency about themselves, as though emerging densely and fully formed from realms not of this usual world and context. That's both necessary to, and part of, the "magic."

Not that rituals actually are divorced from their immediate and more remote contexts; quite the opposite. Rituals are completely creatures of the context in which they take place. (Rhetoricians speak of this "epideictic" quality of ritual speech, for example, but do not seem to know how to explain how it works—or why in fact all language is "epideictic!") But ritual texts manage to draw the context into themselves, because every symbol in a tightly structured ritual gets its specific, "this-ritual" loading for special effectiveness from the overall structure of the text itself. What was externally only wafer and wine are Body and Blood within the ritual spacetime; and, in turn, they constitute "sacrificed" Lamb of God, the "sacrifice" being instanced in their consumption. Ritual symbols, then, are—to borrow the sectarian term—"transubstantiated" from merely ordinary stuff, be it a word or expression, a color, a melody, a movement of people's bodies in a laid-out space. Drawn in from everyday experience to be part of an organized design, the symbols become design elements in an overall figurative portrait or picture (the technical term is *diagram*) of what the text is supposed to effectuate in its particular context.

In this way a ritual text paints a picture of what it accomplishes in relation to that context and *can change our experience of the context* to the degree we accept the picture. And we accept it emotionally as well as otherwise. Recall my earlier discussion of Vygotskij here. A ritual symbolically creates contextually experienced chain-complexes of ideas; how a ritual causes this in those who experience it, even at second hand, is its measure of effectiveness. And it is important to recall that these are intuited ideas—laden with affect or emotion as they hit us—of how people, things, and situations fit together one with another, how they ought to fit together, and how, mystically speaking, they are destined to fit together. Ritually speaking, doesn't every marriage ceremony in our own day turn what began as a chance meeting into predestined wedded couplehood?

In the ritual medium of words in particular, uttering them over speaking time "paints" the ritual "picture." It is just as in music, where the measured ("metrical") organization of tones, singly and in chords, constitutes a rhythmic poetry over the duration of a piece. Or, consider the medium of spatial arrangement of people and things. Here, a ritual "picture" is painted in two ways. First, by the two- or three-dimensional static relative positions of ritually relevant people and things. Second, by their dynamic relative movements in space, if any, over the duration of the ritual. Both words and spatiality are central to the original Lincoln text. Let's look at how they work.

The verbal text of the Gettysburg Address operates, not at the level of syllables, as in poetic doggerel, but in two other features of composition. (I attempt to lay this out visually in the accompanying structural chart of its poetics.) One is the syntactic construction of the sentences. Lincoln accomplishes a kind of incantation by repeating simple forms. This results, cumulatively, in long chains of parallelism, repetition of key words and sets of words that serve as his operant ritual symbols. A second, cumulative effect comes from creating a "fractally" repeating structure—doing the same thing at level upon level upon level of textual form. The text breaks in the middle, at what I have labeled segment [4], "It is altogether fitting and proper that we should do this." This comments, in essence, on the propriety of saying and thereby doing what the speaker, Lincoln, if successful, is in fact doing together with the other people present: "dedicat[ing] a portion of [the Gettysburg battle]field" as a government military cemetery. (Lincoln's early draft of segment [4] is, "This we may, in all propriety do." Pretty lame, though it does serve to break the wonderful repetitive rhythms of [1-3] and [5-6]. The rephrased sentence, with its formulaic <u>altogether</u> <u>fitting</u> <u>and</u> <u>proper</u> and its <u>do</u> <u>this</u> emphasized in a subordinate clause at the very end, reminds one of Christ's injunction to "do this for me." Lincoln takes up, in parallel, what "it is for us" to do in the very complex sixth and final major segment.)

As I noted, ritual text is, at once, completely dependent for its effectiveness on the context in which it occurs, which it "pictorially" attaches to and transforms in some appropriately experienceable way. At the same time, principles of dense internal organization of its symbolic elements give ritual text a semblance of self-sufficient autonomy from its physical context. At Gettysburg, Lincoln anchored his actual performance first to the immediate and proximate context of the cemetery dedication and second to the remoter context of the history and destiny of the nation—at that time under a cloud of uncertainty (just as was his own political future). Seizing on the uncertainty—indeed, making it the overall "to-be-or-not-to-be" theme—he incorporates in his verbal text America's "fathers," its current "honored dead," veterans and soldiers of the battle, as well as his (still living) audience of (perhaps waveringly loyal) other Americans—together with himself—as a totalized ritual "we." He speaks of "[the] nation" in both historical and mystical time: "four score and seven years ago" to "now" in the first part of his remarks, "[the] larger sense" of its futurity being on "the earth" "under God" in the second. In this way, ordinary space and time of history in segments [1-3] are made parallel to the mystical Christian realm in segments [5-6].

Lincoln uses the physical arrangement of the ritual site to organize the relations of all the people named as well as summoned to dedicatory effort. At the schematically apical top-and-center of the site he, Lincoln, "that nation's" Chief Magistrate and Commander-in-Chief, stands to call his audience to its challenge and destiny that are the cruces of the text. Here, the birth/death/re-birth of the political nation (whose shaky government of/by/for the people Lincoln happened to head) and the eternal "endur[ance]" of the nation's soul ("Liberty" or "free-dom" and "equal[ity]") are the issues Lincoln brings together in parallel at the focal point. Yet there at the focal point stands the unpronounced "I" at the center of his enunciated "we:" summoning all the copartici-pants in his text, those named as well as those present, to what the speaker, Abraham Lincoln, stands for in the way of "unfinished work." Because of this double contextualization that Lincoln built in to the perfor-mance, the printed Gettysburg Address still speaks to us with a power rarely equaled in American public rhetoric. As a textually robust ritualization in words, it can even be extracted from its context with its "mes-sage" intact. Certainly Lincoln thought so; he contin-ued to refine the text with minor re-wordings after the event—making it even better as a poetic ritual text—as he several times supplied new handwritten copies for later commemorative distribution.

Let's turn to the mechanics of the text-in-con-text. First, the internal metrical organization of the verbal material, and then how the features of context contribute to these metaphorically chained symbolic equivalences in the overall "message" event.

In Figure 1 I give a diagram of the structures I am talking about, in order to allow you to follow the text and its analysis. I have numbered and lettered the major segments of the text that Lincoln spoke accord-ing to the tiered organization of clause-like units of

[1] *Four score and seven years ago*
  <u>our</u> fathers
           on this continent,
 .a]

 .b] ₪ and
the proposition that
   .1]   *all men*

[2] ₪ *Now*
    <u>we</u> **are engaged in**   a
 .a]   testing
  .a]
  whether
    .1a]
    .2b]
or
    .1]
    .2]
₪ and

[3 .a] <u>We</u> **are met** on   a
          field of
 .b] <u>We</u> [**are met**]/
        have come
  .1]

       a portion of that field,
     as **a final resting place**
for   <u>those</u>
   .a] <u>who</u>   **here**
    .1]that

[4] *It is altogether fitting and proper*
 .a] *that* <u>we</u>

[5a.a]
But,<< *in a larger sense,*

Figure 1.

brought forth

a new nation,

conceived

in *LIBERTY*

DEDICATED TO

are created

₪ *EQUAL.*

great   civil war,

that nation,

<< **any nation**

so conceived

SO DEDICATED

long   ₪ **can...endure.**

great   battle[-]
             that war.

TO DEDICATE

gave their lives

that nation   ≠ ***might live***.

SHOULD DO THIS.

.1]   <u>we</u>
.2]   <u>we</u>
.3]   <u>we</u>

                                    this ground.
.b] <u>The</u> <u>brave</u> <u>men</u>
   .1]

and
   .2]
      .a] <u>who</u>   struggled   *here*
                                            it,

        .a] <u>our</u>
           .1]
or
           .2]
[5b]   <u>The world</u>
   .a.1]
   .a.2] <<
nor
   .a] what
           <u>we</u>   *SAY*   *here*,
but
   .b] ≠ <u>it</u>
      .a] what
           <u>they</u> 🔁 *DID*   *here*.
[6a] *It is for*
           <u>us</u>
rather,
   .1]   *here*

      .a] which
           <u>they</u>
         .1] <u>who</u>   fought   *here*
                    have...advanced.
[6b] *It is... for*
χ rather
           <u>us</u>

CANNOT DEDICATE –
<< CANNOT CONSECRATE –
<< CANNOT HALLOW

living

≠ **dead**

HAVE CONSECRATED

far beyond
≠ **poor power**

to add

≠ [to] detract.

little *will…note*

≠ **long** [*will*] *remember*

>> **never** *can…forget*

the living,

TO BE DEDICATED… TO
the unfinished work

thus far so nobly

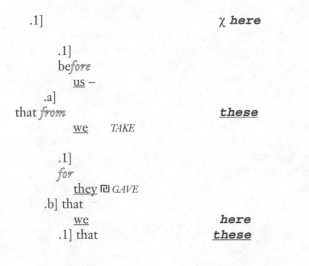

    .1]   χ *here*

    .1]
    be*fore*
     <u>us</u> –
  .a]
that *from*   <u>**these**</u>
    <u>we</u>   *TAKE*

    .1]
    for
     <u>they</u> ₪ *GAVE*
  .b] that
    <u>we</u>   **here**
  .1] that   <u>***these***</u>

  .2] that   this
                      under God,

  .3] and that
    .a]
    .b]
    .c]

                   THE EARTH.

TO BE... DEDICATED TO

the   great   task

remaining

HONORed   **dead**

increased   DEVOTION TO

that **cause**

which

<< the last full measure of   DEVOTION –

highly   RESOLVE

dead

shall...have died

...not...in vain –

nation ,

≠ *shall have a new birth*

of *FREEDOM* –

government

of   the people,

₪ by   the people,

₪ for   the people,   << ***shall not perish from***

.

sentence-structure. At the same time, I have organized the component unit-sized words and expressions of his prose into vertical columns to emphasize what I believe are the remarkable verbal parallelisms, repetitions, and progressions that operate according to their own special effects, much as in poetry, music, and graphic art. Chains of such elements are lined up vertically (as syntax allows), linked by being given similar font and diacritic treatment, to indicate chain-complex equivalence or identity or, for various pairs and triads of terms, special effects like chain-complexes of oppositeness (≠) or complementarity (₪), or semantic crescendo (<<) and decrescendo (>>) effects. (These operate as well at the level of clauses, of course, as marked.) Nevertheless, the chart attempts to preserve the customary left-to-right and top-to-bottom printing conventions so the text can be read normally from beginning to end. Where the rhetorical structure dictates, some material has had to be charted out of the spoken order of denotational text. Accordingly, three dots (...) appear in the place where a word that is elsewhere plotted actually occurs in Lincoln's text (it can generally be located in my chart immediately before the marked gap or, rarely, as the following word in the same clause). The structure will become clearer as we follow along.

Lincoln organizes the whole text into a First Part—Pause—Second Part structure, like a conical figure of two nappes meeting at their vertex (segment [4]). He structures each sentence internally to give maximal rhetorical presence and force to the important concepts. Every sentence starts out, basically, with a simple sentence-subject and simple predicate (with or without a preceding temporal adverbial—like <u>four score</u> <u>and</u> <u>seven years</u> <u>ago</u>—to set up the time frame). Most of the sentences conclude not with a simple noun, but with an appended object or complement construction to which are appended additional modifiers that prolong the basic, simple sentence. As a sentence unfolds in time within the complements or modifiers, a yet further modifying phrase hangs onto modifying phrase in a structurally very rhythmic arrangement that creates a cascading series of memorable, almost autonomous phrases of greatly resonant power.

For example, right in the initial segment, marked [1] in the accompanying figure, we have the simple clause [Subject:] <u>our</u> <u>fathers</u>—[Predicate:] <u>brought</u> <u>forth</u> <u>a</u> <u>new</u> <u>nation</u>. To this Lincoln adds the complex and parallel modifiers explaining what kind of nation they created relevant to the "message" of this occasion. It is a nation, Lincoln declares, [1.a] <u>conceived</u> <u>in</u> <u>liberty</u> (passive participle followed by prepositional phrase), <u>and</u> one [1.b] <u>dedicated</u> <u>to</u> <u>the</u> <u>proposition</u> (again, passive participle followed by prepositional phrase). But which proposition? Another modifier expands, this one a full clause that quotes Mr. Jefferson's immortal text in the Declaration of Independence: <u>the</u> <u>proposition</u> (or truth, we might say) [1.b.1] <u>that</u> <u>all</u> <u>men</u> <u>are</u> <u>created</u> <u>equal</u>. This structure rolls along from beginning to end, unfolding in a way by adding deeper and deeper levels of grammatical structure.

But this principle of composition even intensifies as Lincoln moves from beginning to end. By the text's finale in segment [6], Lincoln lays out in segments [6a] and [6b] the things for us the living to be (here) dedicated to accomplishing so as truly to dedicate the cemetery. Here, his text gets very deeply embedded in syntactic complexity, level after level after level, the last unit [6b.l.b.3.c] resulting from five-fold nesting of phrases within phrases. The unfinished work in [6a] of those who fought at Gettysburg is spelled out in [6b] as *our* great task remaining and it is enumerated in multiple parallel formations, for example [6b.1.a] parallel to [6b.1.b]; within the latter, [6b.1.b.1] parallel to [6b.1.b.2] and to [6b.1.b.3]; and so forth. As each phrase occurring at some level of the complex structure seems to come to completion, we are treated to yet another example of the same principles of composition all over again, as what we thought was the last word bursts open with yet another construction to complete the thought.

So, even considered as a denotational text, a structured message in the informational sense, the whole has what we would now call a "fractal" beauty of structure. Think of the kind of aerial fireworks that, shot up high, bursts open in sequential stages as its remaining parts float down in the sky, each array of color hanging in the air for a moment to dazzle us and then in turn bursting into further, similarly dazzling color. It is the ultimate stuff, placed toward the end of every one of Lincoln's rhetorical segments, that gives the central symbolic oomph to the whole segment and to its import for the whole ritual text.

At the same time, Lincoln develops for each important symbol its proper emphasis in relation to another symbol that he places in parallel to it, making a balanced pair at a relevant position within their respective grammatical phrases: thus even within the first segment, <u>our</u> <u>fathers</u> [agent subject]—<u>all</u> <u>men</u> [patient subject] and <u>brought</u> <u>forth</u> [active]—<u>are</u> <u>cre-ated</u> [passive] are two pairs in tandem, like mirror-images nicely rounding out the two full clauses of [1]; <u>conceived</u> (in)—<u>dedicated</u> (to) participial phrases used in describing the United States; <u>liberty</u>—<u>equal</u>[ity] each as its phrase-culminating value we get from the nation's founding fraternity.

More importantly, note also what we can term Lincoln's cantillation with tremolo on particular ritual points central to his "message"—his elaborate, decorative emphasis of them by repetition (that we can see in the vertical columnar array of Figure 1). Through rep-etition-with-variation, the basic principle of poetic parallelism, Lincoln highlighted certain words and phrases as the vehicles of the central symbols of this ritual (<u>a</u> <u>new</u> <u>nation</u> [1] > <u>that</u> <u>nation</u> [2.a.a.1.a]—<u>any</u> <u>nation</u> [so conceived ...] [2.a.a.1.b] > <u>that</u> <u>nation</u> [3.b.1.a.1]; <u>this</u> <u>nation</u>" [6b.1.b.2]. (Here, also note the culminative progression, <u>a</u> > <u>that</u> [parenthetical <u>any</u>] > <u>that</u> > <u>this</u>, getting ultimately to the ritual "here-and-now" <u>nation</u> that matters.) In several places, Lincoln repeats exactly the same linguistic forms with poeti-cally new meanings each time—punning in a way that seizes our attention: <u>conceived</u> <u>in</u> [1.a] vs. <u>so</u> <u>conceived</u> [2.a.a.1.a] plays on the senses of reproduction vs. ratio-nal thought, figuratively making the key point about what differentiates this nation from others. Again, <u>dedicated</u> (<u>to</u>) [1.b; 2.a.a.2.b.2] vs. <u>to</u> <u>dedicate</u> [3.b.1;

5a.a.1] plays on the difference between goal-orientation vs. ritually setting aside or <u>consecrat</u>[ing] [5a.a.2; 5a.b]. Observe how the two senses are merged and figuratively equated, with passive construction, in Lincoln's twice calling for "us" to dedicate ourselves— that is, for us ourselves <u>to</u> <u>be</u> <u>dedicated</u> <u>to</u> [6a.1; 6b.1]—<u>the</u> <u>unfinished</u> <u>work</u> of the <u>great</u> <u>civil</u> <u>war</u> and thus of <u>this</u> <u>nation</u>. He also uses whole series or sequences of words and phrases closely related in meaning to create the framework of overall metaphors in which his ritual theme is established: (the nation's) *birth* in history > (for humans,) actual or (for the nation,) threatened *death* > *rebirth* in *or* to (human) *immortality* or (national) cosmic eternity.

Lincoln's progressions of nested repetitions first zoom in relentlessly within the spatial realm, like a camera focusing us down, down, down; it is a field of meaning made orderly in the very textual order of the ritual: <u>this</u> <u>continent</u> [1] > <u>a</u> <u>great</u> <u>battlefield</u> [3.a] > <u>a</u> <u>portion</u> <u>of</u> <u>that</u> <u>field</u> and <u>a</u> <u>final</u> <u>resting</u> <u>place</u> (i.e., 'graves') [3.b.1] > <u>here</u> [3.b.l.a]. In this first half of the ritual text, he is tracing events in historical time as well, first the founding of the nation on a principle or proposition; then the "testing" of that principle or proposition—note how an exception "proves," i.e., tests, a rule or timeless generalization—by the war that is the ongoing reality; then the actual immediate present of the occasion itself, face-to-face with the dead and with each other. What to say or do *now*?

Quite brilliantly, in the second half of the ritual, Lincoln precipitously zooms out again, though always anchored in the "here-and-now" he shares with his addressees, until he makes the physical ground part, in the larger sense, of the cosmic eternal of God's—not merely humanity's—earth: this ground [5a.a] > here and it [5a.b.a] (> 8 times here or equivalent) > this nation under God [6b.1.b.2] > the earth [6b.1.b.3]. Lincoln starts from the "here-and-now" he had reached at the end of the first part, and draws it up not into mere human futurity, though to be sure he appeals to his audience in terms of what it is for [them] to do after the ceremonial occasion. His call is, rather, for the rebirth of the freedom articulated in the Declaration of Independence, that is, for *the sacred futurity of an eternal principle*. This abstract value will not perish from the earth nor will this nation, under God, in that sacred order if the audience will only dedicate themselves to carrying on with the great task remaining before us in the temporal order. The audience will thereby join in the cosmic category he creates in this very ritual text, one that includes the Revolutionary Era fathers, the Civil War Era dead soldiers now buried "here," those (here) still living, and most of all the very individual who is grammatically at the center of and focused upon by the little inclusive word "*we*:" the speaker, Abraham Lincoln himself, their Commander-in-Chief, their Chief Magistrate, their Executive, their President.

We can note these poetic progressions independent of any overall "logic" rhetoricians want to find in the text—it's technically merely an exhortation to greater resolve in the war effort, now figuratively wrapped in eternal principle. The whole emergent text moves through two familiar orders, the temporal and the eternal, manipulating symbols that draw people and events in the first order together with forces and destinies in the second. So we can see why certain things are constantly repeated and embellished through the whole text to show that they retain their essence in both realms. Such are, for example, <u>Liberty</u> [1.a] and <u>equal</u>[ity] [1.b.1] at the initial, conceptual and dedicatory founding moment of the <u>new</u> <u>nation</u>. These are recuperated in the cosmic realm of eternity at the very end by "our" resolution to give a <u>new</u> <u>birth</u> to <u>freedom</u> [6b.1.b.2].

Again, note the fractal structure of repetitions in positioning expressions for the United States, its history, its destiny. In segment [1], <u>a</u> <u>new</u> <u>nation</u>, a specific thing, is dedicated to the equality of <u>all</u> <u>men</u> [1.b.1], in the realm of general concepts; in [2], precisely parallel, the fate of <u>that</u> <u>nation</u> [2.a.a.1a]—specific—is linked to the fate of <u>any</u> <u>nation</u> [2.a.a.2b]—general—similarly conceived and dedicated. The whole first part, the historical recitation of events, concludes with Lincoln, using the modal <u>might</u>, making contingent the continuing life of <u>that</u> <u>nation</u> [3.b.1.a.1], the one whose history has been recited in outline from founding to Civil War to the Gettysburg battle to the precarious "now." Here is the crux of the moment to hand.

Then, in the second part, where Lincoln is speaking in the "larger sense" of futurities of the sacred and eternal, he repeatedly uses exactly the same structure of contrasts of specific and general. In [5a] and [5b], this same opposition is twice nested. <u>We</u> in [5a.a] and <u>the</u> <u>brave</u> <u>men</u> (<u>who</u> <u>struggled</u> <u>here</u>) in

[5.a.b] in each sub-part of [5a] draws a contrast
between us, the living, more this-worldly, and the
dead, now become eternal (buried, they have joined
"our fathers"). As a higher-level unit, [5a] as a whole,
dealing with these specific actors in the nation's present moment, is contrasted with [5b], which is framed
by how <u>the</u> <u>world</u>—a generalized actor—is presumed
to evaluate the contrast in [5a]. The significant difference the world will understand is between <u>what</u> <u>we</u> <u>say</u>
<u>here</u> [5b.a.a], feebly trying, with words, to dedicate an
earth(l)y memorial, and <u>what</u> <u>they</u> <u>did</u> <u>here</u> [5b.a.b],
succeeding, with deeds, in consecrating it for eternity.

    Segment [6a] takes up the theme of [5a] once
more: since our words alone will not succeed in <u>dedi-</u>
<u>cat</u>[ing] <u>this</u> <u>ground</u> [5a.a], rather we must dedicate
ourselves, i.e., we must <u>be</u> <u>dedicated</u> [6a.1], to com-
pleting what <u>they</u> <u>who</u> <u>fought</u> <u>here</u> [6a.1.a.1] <u>struggled</u>
[5a.b.2.a] to do. This specific <u>unfinished</u> <u>work</u> [6a.1]—
which the crowd, in context, must have understood to
be the cause of the Union—is in parallel fashion ele-
vated in [6b] to <u>the</u> <u>great</u> <u>task</u> <u>remaining</u> <u>before</u> <u>us</u>
[6b.1] in a generalized eternal realm. Being dedicated
to the specific is, in parallel fashion, equated to being
dedicated to the general—to the cosmic fate of <u>these</u>
<u>dead</u> [6b.1.b.1], of <u>this</u> <u>nation</u> [, <u>under</u> <u>God</u>,]
[6b.1.b.2], and of a principle of <u>government</u> [6b.1.b.3],
all of which Lincoln anchors to the very site: "here,"
where "we," the living make the dead immortal.
Within the last segment [6b.1.b] that calls Lincoln's
audience to purposive resolve, note yet again the
three-part crescendo of abstractness in the parallelism:
[6b.1.b.1] is a resolve to redeem the specific fact of the

soldiers' deaths; [6b.1.b.2] is a resolve for the resurrection of <u>freedom</u> in <u>this nation, under God</u> (whose conception <u>in Liberty</u> is recalled from [1.a]); while [6b.1.b.3] is a resolve to render eternal the abstract principle, given in the ringing phrase (borrowed and refashioned from many earlier writers) <u>government of the people, by the people, for the people</u> which, then, <u>shall not perish from the earth</u>.

But the two major parts of the text work similarly. Lincoln recounts in [1] to [3] the whole set of *historical*—and therefore specific—precedents for being at Gettysburg on that November day. In [5] and [6] respectively, he turns to the set of first *moral* and then, additively, *performative* contingencies and futurities, the ones that depend upon and would follow on Lincoln's success at forging a resolute "*we*." These futurities can be made real—can be made consecrated flesh, as it were—only if the ritual is successful, if it draws its speaker and addressees together in the unity it declares.

Here, then, we come to the most remarkable of the sustained parallelisms of repetition in Lincoln's text, clearly the central axis of what the ritual pronouncement is all about: our "<u>dedicat</u>[ing]" and our "<u>be</u>[ing] <u>dedicated</u>." Six times Lincoln repeats it in one or another grammatical form, with one or another special sense. Twice more he repeats it in the synonym 'devote' (as in the wonderful opposition of our *tak*[ing] <u>devotion</u> [6b.1.a] from the dead's having *giv*[en] <u>the last full measure of devotion</u> [6b.1.a.1]). He elaborates it in the brilliant verbal crescendo <u>dedicate</u> << <u>consecrate</u> << <u>hallow</u> [5.a.a.1,2,3; 5.a.b]. And—if the audi-

ence or reader has any doubts left about the ritual task
he is summoning us to—he spells it out in the explicitly defining performative formula for how, in democ-
ratic assembly, <u>the</u> <u>people</u> take binding action: <u>we</u> <u>here</u>
<u>highly</u> <u>resolve</u> (<u>that</u>…) [6b.1.b (.1,.2,.3)].

Observe the progression. In [1-3], <u>dedicate</u>
keeps its active voice, but shifts between [1-2]—where
the meaning is commitment to an eternal truth—and
[3]—where the ongoing ritual event is named as a
<u>dedicat</u>[ion] [3.b.1], a setting-aside, the doing of
which, in [4], Lincoln judges to be <u>altogether</u> <u>fitting</u>
<u>and</u> <u>proper</u>. In [5-6], note, the earlier punning disjunc-
tion is made clearer <u>in</u> [the] <u>larger</u> <u>sense</u>. First, if we
cannot <u>dedicate</u>…<u>this</u> <u>ground</u> [5a.a], i.e., set it aside,
we certainly cannot <u>consecrate</u> it [5a.a.2], i.e., really
and truly commit it to the sacred eternal, as clergy or
similar Christian religious officiants would do. Nor
certainly can we <u>hallow</u> it [5a.a.3], i.e., make it sacred
in the first place, which only God can do. Notice that
those who fought in the Battle of Gettysburg are said
to be such <u>consecrat</u>[ors] of the cemetery ground
[5a.b]; they have already committed it to the sacred
eternal. In fighting or <u>struggl</u>[ing] <u>here</u>, they have
done holy—if <u>unfinished</u>—<u>work</u> [6a.1] that <u>the</u>
<u>world</u>…<u>can</u> <u>never</u> <u>forget</u> [5b.b], i.e., that is enduring.

Now we can see Lincoln's extraordinary and
priestly Eucharistic move in segment [6]: if we cannot
really and truly <u>dedicate</u>—active voice—in that enduring and eternal realm, we can <u>be</u> <u>dedicated</u> <u>here</u> [6a.1]
in it—passive voice form meaning just 'committed to'
something. Now in the parallel segment [6b.1],
Lincoln uses the formal figure of chiasmus, crisscross-

ing, as he takes the passive form and returns it to its ritual or performative meaning. Observe the changed orderings: It is for us…rather…to be dedicated here to … [6a.1] vs. It is rather for us to be here dedicated to … [6b.1]. As in the service of the Eucharist, we must become transformed and mystically *set aside to (and within) "[the] cause"*—that is, incorporatively dedicated to it—by tak[ing] increased devotion (like wine and wafer transubstantiated) from the martyrs who gave the last full measure of devotion. Thus, our high resol[ution] to make it so that they martyred themselves for *our* cause—the cause of this nation, under God and its new birth of freedom (a *re-birth* recuperating 1776), this cause that "we" can here-and-now make immortal and eternal, never perish[ing] from the earth.

Indeed, there truly is a quality of Shakespearean seriousness to Lincoln's puns and plays on words! He was a highly gifted miniaturist in words as he moves across the realms of meaning that a single word-form can have, and as he plays upon the significant differences of the various grammatical forms of those very words.

But to appreciate further this masterpiece of "message"ing, we must imagine the scene on that November day. (If you've been to the site recently, you will know that the cemetery has now been enveloped in large-scale Gettysburg Battle tourism that decreases the contemplative sacredness of the site, instead emphasizing the battle itself.) Imagine an open-fan, a semicircular-shaped cemetery sloping down-and-out from near the top of a knoll or ridge. Imagine pie-

piece sections of graves for the various states' dead in various stages of completion or in-process freshness. At the radial center of this semicircular array was a flagpole, temporarily in the position where a large war monument was later erected (dedicated, 1869), barely beyond the closest-in circumferential lines of then-fresh graves. Slightly higher up, on the grounds of an already existing cemetery—the site was known as Cemetery Hill—there was set up a platform for speakers and dignitaries, leaving room for the audience between it and the new National Cemetery. In effect, on the surface of the hill all this comprised a somewhat lengthened and inverted (convex rather than concave) amphitheatre, all oriented to a high center-point of interest, where the speakers' and dignitaries' platform was set up. The speakers looked out from that center to the audience and beyond, to the places of burial of the dead. In the converse direction, the dead lay beneath the earth at the backs of the audience, who faced forward toward the center where Everett and Lincoln and others spoke to them and enjoined of them dedication to the completion of <u>the unfinished</u> <u>work</u> <u>which</u> <u>they</u> <u>who</u> <u>fought</u> <u>here</u> [lying behind the audience; constituting their background] <u>have</u> <u>thus</u> <u>far</u> <u>so</u> <u>nobly</u> <u>advanced</u>.

We can note in the address the way that the system of what are technically called "deictic" categories—the way one uses <u>this</u>es and <u>that</u>s; the way one speaks of a "past," a "present" and a realm of futurity; the way one refers to what is <u>here</u> and to what is <u>there</u>—is masterfully used by Lincoln (who even revised the text after the fact to make it better, that is, tighter in its ritual poetics of deixis). The national past, the bloody and immediately deadly present, and the destiny Lincoln and his audience (and successors) will shape is verbally put into correspondence with the shape of the physical array in which the address is delivered: <u>fathers</u> metaphorically rolling up from the mythical past; <u>honored</u> <u>dead</u>, lying in graves just downhill and all around behind us; <u>us</u> <u>the</u> <u>living</u>, arrayed inside the concentric rings of the cemetery being dedicated; and the focal point we all seek in the nation's future, starting behind the audience and marching up to the high-ground top-and-center point of the audience's gaze where Lincoln himself stands, speaking to them. As in any good sacred ritual, the cosmic axis—here, leading us to redemption by (re)dedication and rebirth—runs right through the position that Lincoln speaks from, so that the futurity is indeed the mystical futurity of that <u>larger</u> <u>sense</u> in which we are <u>here</u> [very much on <u>this</u> <u>ground</u> as well as, in mystical nationalist time, <u>on</u> <u>this</u> <u>continent</u> and <u>the</u> <u>earth</u>] not so much to <u>dedicate</u>, as <u>to</u> be <u>dedicated</u>, punning on the official-collective ceremony vs. the personal-spiritual meaning of the ceremonial transformation. Compare here again the Eucharistic service, in which, inscribing the figure of a cross—The Cross—in ceremonial action, one incorporates the sacred Body and Blood so as to be mystically incorporated into the Body made institutional in the church and among its congregation of worshippers.

We can now appreciate even more the subtlety with which Lincoln uses such deixis. In [1], a past tense verb, <u>brought</u> <u>forth</u>, describes the founding

actions of the <u>fathers</u> of <u>a</u> <u>new</u> <u>nation</u> at the far end of
the time interval of 87 years before the moment of
speaking. In [2], a present form of an inherently con-
tinuous verb, <u>are</u> <u>engaged</u> <u>in</u>, describes the ongoing
frame of <u>a</u> <u>great</u> <u>civil</u> <u>war</u>, implicating its habitualness
or surround of the moment of speaking, hence <u>now</u>.
In [3], a present perfect, <u>are</u> <u>met</u>/<u>have</u> <u>come</u>, describing a resultative state of an action, brings us, still
within "now," to "here." Observe that in this first,
recitational half of the text, each time something is
introduced—for example, <u>a</u> <u>new</u> <u>nation</u> in [1], the next
time Lincoln holds it up he does so with <u>that</u>, the dis-
tal demonstrative appropriate to setting things out for
contemplation at a distance.

   In his text-dividing sentence, [4], Lincoln uses
a present tense and the verb <u>do</u> <u>this</u>, with the proximal
demonstrative, that substitutes for the whole complex
phrase of [3.b.1] (...<u>to</u> <u>dedicate</u>...<u>might</u> <u>live</u>).

   Then in the second half, in [5] and [6],
Lincoln moves out from "here" and "now" into contingent futurities, futurities that depend on our orient-
ing ourselves to the deontological lessons of the
recitation of the first segment. At this point, Lincoln
switches entirely into the "proximal" deictics, <u>here</u>,
<u>this</u>/<u>these</u>, <u>we</u>; he has now brought everything he
denotes inside the ritual precinct. So, we start from
the impossibility of really <u>doing</u> <u>this</u>, i.e., dedicating,
consecrating, or hallowing *<u>this</u>* <u>ground</u> by merely
<u>say</u>[ing] something (as opposed to the soldiers' having
done something!). We learn that we *can* in effect <u>do</u>
<u>this</u> by ourselves <u>being</u> <u>dedicated</u> to joining Lincoln in
the "we" who will bring about actual futurities, all

wonderfully laid out as such in parallel future constructions that are thus made ritually equivalent—an
emotion-filled chain-complex of ideals—in [6b.1.b]:
that [the dead] <u>shall</u> <u>not</u> <u>have</u> <u>died</u> <u>in</u> <u>vain</u> = that [the
U.S.A.] <u>shall</u> <u>have</u> <u>a</u> <u>new</u> <u>birth</u> <u>of</u> <u>freedom</u> = that [the
principle of democratic government] <u>shall</u> <u>not</u> <u>perish</u>
<u>from</u> <u>the</u> <u>earth</u>. The proximal demonstratives
<u>this</u>/<u>these</u>—<u>here</u> combined with implied and actual
future forms give us a presentational effect, holding
before the ritual participants the very outcomes of a
successful performance.

The Myth is the "Message"

As I observed, "[t]he world will little note, nor long remember" what Edward Everett said in his Gettysburg "Oration." But the mythology surrounding Lincoln's "Dedicatory Remarks" celebrates them as a rhetorical triumph of the quintessentially "American" civil-religious voice, and it celebrates Lincoln as the people's evangelist for the Union cause. As this very constructed "message" had already been helpful to his initial election, it was all the more definitively elaborated at his death. Each of the various mythological strands indicates something interesting about the "message"-worthiness of the Gettysburg Address.

There are various myths about the text's composition. The one I was told in elementary school was that Lincoln quickly jotted it on the back of an envelope while waiting at the train station, or while on the train to Gettysburg. There are variant details: that it was composed after dinner in the Wills house the night before its delivery; or, early in the morning before its delivery; or, partly in Washington and partly at Gettysburg. Or even that the text was only partially written out, the rest coming spontaneously from Lincoln in an inspired burst of feeling at the dedication ceremony itself. The absence of a definitive reading manuscript in Lincoln's hand that matches the stenographic record of a reporter reinforces the sense of these words as more or less divinely inspired and spoken by a priest if not prophet. These accounts, to different degrees, imbue the text with the sincerity of inspired, spontaneous words-of-the-moment that, like all good poetry, are supposed in a kind of Romantic view to come to the inspired poet fluently and directly in an inspiration—like the feelings of religious conversion and ecstasy that they allude to.

But in actuality, Lincoln had long since formulated the general metaphorical structure of the Gettysburg text: the providential delivery of the Union to "us" on the 4th of July, the birthday of the nation, upon principles of universal human rights (notwithstanding the later Constitutional compromises about slavery). Already on the evening of the 7th of July in 1863, just a few days after the Gettysburg and Vicksburg engagements, Lincoln extemporaneously spoke to a crowd outside the Executive Mansion on this subject. His words were stenographically reported as follows:

> How long ago is it—eighty odd years—since on the Fourth of July for the first time in the history of the world a nation by its representatives, assembled and declared as a self-evident truth that "all men are created equal." That was the birthday of the United States of America....
> [A]nd on the 4th [just passed] the cohorts of those who opposed the declaration that all men are created equal "turned tail" and ran. Gentlemen, this is a glorious theme, and the occasion for a speech, but I am not prepared to make one worthy of the occasion. I would like to speak in terms of praise due to the many brave officers and soldiers who have fought in the cause of the Union and liberties of the country from the beginning of the war.

Even earlier, when the war was in its initial phases, Lincoln had sent a message to a special session of Congress on 4 July 1861, in which many of the phrasings of the Gettysburg remarks can already be noted. Addressing the Confederacy's secession, Lincoln argues that

> this issue embraces more than the fate of these United States. It presents to the whole family of man the question, whether a constitutional republic, or democracy—a Government of the people by the same people—can or cannot maintain its territorial integrity against its own domestic foes. It presents the question, whether discontented individuals... can... put an end to free government upon the earth.

Lincoln rhetorically asks why, in contrast to the ideals for which he—and, he hopes, Congress—stand, the Confederate declaration of independence "omit[s] the words 'all men are created equal', and why their constitution omits the phrase 'We, the People': Why this deliberate pressing out of view of the rights of men and the authority of the people?" And he concludes by remarking that even "[a]s a private citizen, the Executive [=President] could not have consented that these institutions [of popular government] shall perish"; and much less can he do so as President.

So it was not merely the issues that were Lincoln's to articulate; the very images of a "message" had long been forming themselves in phrasings that he ultimately put together in the brilliant poetry of his text of November 1863. While that text may have gotten a final pre-delivery polishing in the days before the 19th, it certainly was in far advanced draft by a week or so before, when Lincoln was studying the layout of the cemetery and reviewing the text of Everett's oration.

Then there is the myth of the audience's stunned—or indifferent—silence at the dedication, and of Lincoln's sense of the immediate failure of the speech. Just as the myth of whole-sprung, inspired composition (or extemporaneity) hints at the "message" of Lincoln's powerful evangelical fervor, so this one constructs the image of the overlooked treasure—perhaps like Christ's disregarded message?—proffered to an initially uncomprehending world. (But the world ultimately discovers its treasure and grants immortality to the message.)

Actually, upon delivery, the speech was interrupted five times for applause, at what we can see are all "right" places, as well as receiving sustained applause at its conclusion. The Associated Press stenographer notes applause after [1], when Lincoln quotes the Declaration; after [5a], for the consecrating acts of the brave men... who struggled here; after [5b], contrasting what they did here to our mere verbiage; after [6a], noting that the combatants have thus far... nobly carried on the nation's unfinished work [changed to nobly advanced in later, post-delivery manuscripts]; after [6b.b.1], resolving that these dead shall not have died in vain; and at the end, after shall not perish from the earth, the correspondent noting "long continued applause." All these noted, in spite of recollected memories of silence, whether hostile, uncomprehending, or whatever.

But of course the myths tell us something about the folk notion of the differences between the plain- and brief-spoken Lincoln, President of the people, speaking in language for the people, hoping to be reelected by the people, and the distinguished and Brahmanical public servant and Harvard president, Mr. Everett, who represents the gifts of elite artistry in the heroic Hellenic mold. (The very next day, Ambassador Everett wrote compliments to Lincoln, saying, "I should be glad if I could flatter myself that I came so near the central idea of the occasion in two hours as you did in two minutes." To this, the gracious Lincoln—ever the master of compactly witty words—replied, "In our respective parts yesterday, you could not have been excused to make a short address, nor I a long one.") When successful "message" wraps the message-bearer in its folds like a draped flag, the myth becomes the message. Lincoln's dedicatory remarks became "*The* Gettysburg Address" and this aspect of his "message"—what was at stake "in [the] larger sense" in both the war and *him being President*—was completely off bounds in the particularly rough political season ahead. The verbal and cartoon attacks on Lincoln from the militant northern Abolitionist side or the side of compromise with the Confederacy were sustained and vicious until the 1864 elections and beyond. But he had managed to inhabit a "message" at Gettysburg that, in his eventual martyrdom-to-"that cause" down to the present, seems "not [to have] perish[ed] from the earth."

Homer Simpson Goes to Washington

From the mystical realms of Lincoln's "message" in American memory, let's come back down to earth. Let's look at the "message" of our current Chief Magistrate, a.k.a. "W." How has he managed "message" as a candidate and office-holder? Let's start with his relationship to language and communication. What do people expect verbally nowadays of a person in such a position of responsibility? If Lincoln's best "message" moments resonated with a Christian evangelical plain-style, what do Mr. Bush's best "message" moments resonate with? What does this say about the central workings of our political system?

The current President, the press reports, thinks he has moved up from the Texas Rangers and Harken Oil to head the country's largest diversified corporation, the United States government, of which he is the Chairman and CEO. (This was how reporters contemporaneously characterized Mr. Reagan's style of presidency, too.) How does such a man talk? How did he talk as a candidate who appealed to enough of the electorate that the Supreme Court's right-thinking offensive line decided—5-to-4—to propel him bodily into the presidential end-zone?

Here's a small sample of one-liners recorded during his 2000 candidacy. In one sense, they address what we might understand to be a range of very important current "issues" then—and now—facing American society. Observe:

"The vast majority of our imports come from outside the country."

"Republicans understand the importance of bondage between a mother and a child."

"The Holocaust was an obscene period in our nation's history—I mean in this century's history. But we all lived in this century. I didn't live in this century."

"We have a firm commitment to NATO; we are a part of NATO. We have a firm commitment to Europe; we are a part of Europe."

"When I have been asked who caused the riots and the killing in LA, my answer has been direct and simple: Who is to blame for the riots? The rioters are to blame. Who is to blame for the killings? The killers are to blame."

"We are ready for any unforeseen event that may or may not occur."

"A low voter turnout is an indication of fewer people going to the polls."

"It isn't the pollution that's harming our environment. It's the impurities in our air and water that are doing it."

"Quite frankly, teachers are the only profession that teach our children."

"[It's] time for the human race to enter the solar system."

"Verbosity leads to unclear, inarticulate things."

"Well, I think if you say you're going to do something and don't do it, that's trustworthiness."

"I believe we are on an irreversible trend toward more freedom and democracy—but that could change."

"If we don't succeed, we run the risk of failure."

This stuff looks like political parody, scripted perhaps for *Saturday Night Live*. It ranges hilariously over the whole gag kitbag. Double-talk, malapropisms, the worst hack bromides, logical—denotational—non-sequiturs and redundancies, semantic ignorance of one or another sort, and on and on. At times, the speaker wants to correct himself, but, like verbal slapstick, gets bollixed up even worse. And yet it is very appealing in its own way, is it not? It is, I shall argue—or, rather, the man speaking it is—"on message" in the sociopolitical context in which this conceptual dross—like the stuff of the bumper sticker—happens.

But there's the key point. It's conceptual dross, to be sure. But it has been consistently delivered with a manly tone of conviction, even aggressiveness; with a firm-jawed, non-sissy Texas style of pronunciation that Poppy never really mastered; and with a facial and whole bodily posture of earnestness that has got to make our hearts go out to the guy: he's really, really attempting to grasp things—whatever they are—with his whole being. What has been really trying to the "conceptualizing elites" who criticize him is that Dubya has successfully projected, and successfully continues to project, determination, "*really trying.*" (When his candidacy first surfaced, it seemed to me that Dubya in fact combined attributes of both Ronald Reagan and Dan Quayle. He was like mellow Reagan for projecting principled determination, though without the clarity of Reagan's global anti-Communist slogans Dubya has had only free-enterprise, anti-government slogans to captivate the Reagan Republicrats while doing the bidding of corporate interests in oil, energy, etc. who have invested in his candidacy and then administration. He was like youthful Quayle for lowering expectations to those of the C-minus legacy child, though in a more robustly acceptable way in its new, Texas version.)

When he was tapped by the RNC to rush The Presidency (bigger than Yale's Skull and Bones but—under Dubya—yet more secretive!), he was probably reassured that he himself would not have to face intractables like Middle East foreign policy—much less the twin rubbleheaps of a physically attacked America and a gutted American economy. (But don't worry; the servants—Dick, Rummie, Condie and all—will take care of it, as they always have.) So in the campaign the important "message" was to hold out the promise of change of administrations from smooth, Slick Willie, the "in-yo'-face" Know-It-All. Reverting to the uncouthness from whence *he* sprung, Pimp Willie succumbed to the fleshly temptations of his position of power. For a long, drawn-out time the state of his affairs became the embarrassing center-piece of our affairs of state. And poor Al Gore, by contrast, turned himself into Mr. Know-It-All-Without-(Extramarital-) Lust-in-His-Heart. For Gore, it became increasingly difficult even to keep people convinced that he had the fire-in-the-belly as well. But George W. Bush: earnest in his sincerity, so seemingly ingenuous in his platitudes and gaffes—as well as deflectively proclaiming born-again Christian redemption from sex, drugs, and rock 'n' roll—he was—and, when "on message," still is—really trying. There's hope (and not as in "The Man from ___"). This guy—as well as things—can get better, if he and especially we really try. And we can have a non-Clinton without all those issues, issues, issues and those speeches written and delivered like policy mem-oranda.

So look at the quotes again. They are the stuff of someone who is trying to touch issues, but is some-what uncomfortable, as well as unfamiliar, with the details of them. Missing is the detail of how one in fact gets from first principles through a chain of informed inference to a conclusion. Missing is the detail of technical and other memo-words that live in those places where the gears of actual administration turn. Missing is the detail of factual knowledge of tables of organization and of the functioning of the things in the political, economic, social, and even nat-ural worlds. Someone who communicates this way communicates concern—"really trying"—but not expertise; command, as it were, but not control.

Control over detail is precisely what middle management does, in the corporate world. They're the ones who know how to write contracts in the detail sufficient to execute the deal made higher up with a handshake. They're the ones who know how to draw up tiered organizational plans, modularizing the tasks to get a large job done. They're the ones who know how to look things up like the market projections for raw materials, labor, transportation, etc. and compute the parameters of profit. They're even the ones, it turns out, who know how to disguise losses in the accounts, to find arguable loopholes in those loose regulatory laws, and to apply science in *de facto* if not *de jure* dangerous and harmful ways.

That's *not* what this language of Candidate and now President W projects; just the opposite. It's Homer Simpson's kind of language, or, for older television generations, Ralph Cramden's or Chester A. Riley's. (But Dubya is spouting his verbiage from an inherited, hence familiar position of privilege, and looking forward to even more.) He's *really trying*, and that's fine. Or at least good enough, in this all too imperfect world. We've seen what happens when the underprivileged and oversexed Mr. Know-It-Alls get power! (So poor Al Gore. As his axis of self-differentiation from Mr. Clinton, poor Al Gore bumblingly hints at middle-aged sexuality, no less—even if faithful within marriage—polishing all the while the Mr. Know-It-All image, precisely what the upwardly mobile Mr. Clinton, as President, seemed to have usurped from middle management!)

Take That!

Middle management, professional people, and their press and media—Hey! That's us!—make fun of such folks in CEO and Chairman of the Board positions behind their backs. And we make fun of these kinds of political candidates and officeholders in public. Where *do* they get off taking up such positions? We get the queasy feeling from hearing people who talk like W that the infelicities, the lack of command even of a "standard" register of English, speak volumes about other aspects of such a person's being. For the large number of people whose command of, even virtuosity with, such language is part of their daily lives—for example the means by which, at work, they earn their living—talking this way bespeaks, say, ignorance, and/or pretension and/or stupidity and/or a particular déclassé group-membership, etc. etc. So folks like Dubya become fair game for jokes that emphasize the unseemliness of the perhaps blind, dumb luck that makes those behind—below—beholden to them and highly embarrassed so to be.

In a January, 2001, issue of *The New Yorker*, for example, the *Doonesbury* cartoonist Gary Trudeau observed in relation to then President-Elect Bush:

> My suspicion is that the Bushes' seeming antipathy for me stems from a certain traitor-to-his-class incomprehension. Because, on paper, I'm one of them [Yale]. Anyway, it's true the election result is good for me.
> Bush is this stable, hard target. It's as if Quayle had won. Plus you have the wonderful narrative of how

he got where he now is. It took his brother, his
father, his father's friends, the Florida secretary of
state, and the Supreme Court to pull it off. His
entire life gives fresh meaning to the phrase
"assisted living."

As you see, Mr. Trudeau emphasizes the inert-
ness, the helplessness of the privileged scion: "a stable
hard target. It's as if Quayle had won." People like him
concluded that Mr. Bush's featured demographics
heightened each other—coddled Texas oil-man over-
laid on clubby, Ivy-League "legacy child" of poor
mental endowments—so as to produce an embarrassing specimen at the head of our government.
Aggressive, if ignorant, only wannabe hillbilly mas-
culinity (as opposed to Mr. Clinton's genuinely
upward-struggling—and therefore respectable—kind).
Such a guy can clearly never be concerned with what
the anxious intellectual bourgeoisie thinks is important.

Likewise, here's a bit of what was circulating
on the internet in earlier days of the Bush presidency.
At least it's some of what circulated to me:

Al Gore and George Bush had breakfast together
before their meeting in D.C. last week. The waitress greeted them and asked for their order. Gore
said he'd have oatmeal and applesauce. Bush asked
for a quickie. The waitress glared at him and
stalked off. Gore leaned over and said quietly,
"That's quiche."

***

George W. was asked if he knew what *Roe vs. Wade*
was. He replied: "I think it was the decision that

George Washington had to make before crossing the Delaware."

***

Queen Elizabeth II and Mr. Bush are riding toward Buckingham Palace in an open, 17th century coach hitched to six magnificent, matching white horses. As they proceed, waving to the thousands of cheering Brits lining the streets, the right rear horse lets fly with a horrendous, eye-smarting blast of flatulence. Uncomfortable, but under control, the two heads of state do their best to ignore the whole incident.

But the Queen, seeking to reassure her guest with a down-to-earth genuineness, turns to Mr. Bush and explains, "Mr. President, please accept my regrets; I'm sure you understand that there are some things that even a Queen cannot control."

Ever the gentleman, Mr. Bush replies, "Your Majesty, please don't give the matter another thought. You know, if you hadn't said something, I would have thought it was one of the horses."

So real men—as opposed to Democrats—do like quickies? So feminism's empowering moment, the equivalent of Gay Liberation's "Stonewall," goes unrecognized and—unlike the quickie—unloved? So prairie-patty gentility is offered in return for a royal gesture of reassurance? Look at the unflattering image of Mr. Bush posed by such material. In each case it involves a kind of verbally-cued oafishness and ignorance: an inability to read and recognize the referent of a sophisticated word; unfamiliarity with the legal case-caption that points to one of the key issues of the last half century; unfamiliarity with truly genteel verbal cues of politeness in context. These translate as:

unfit to be taken out to a fancy restaurant; unfit to do more than make a schoolboy stab at critical knowledge underlying issues; unfit to be with *real* royalty (a supposedly distant cousin, no less!), and hence unfit to represent his country.

Perhaps the most telling in this respect are the cleverly doctored images that have made their way to the computer screens of the "knowledge workers" around the world. Here are two that circulated early in W's term of office—both, unsurprisingly, on the same, recurrent theme.

Oh shit, he is even dumber than I thought.

Figure 2.

Figure 3.

Communicating (in a) Democracy

But it is not just the chardonnay, Brie, and quiche set who have been disturbed by the significant amount of truth in these jokes, to judge even from the small sample of quotes above. There is, after all, malicious partisanship in them, and after all, the Clintons and their Democratic ilk have spent years kowtowing to the *grande bourgeoisie* of torrential cash flow on both coasts, those mighty of the metaphorical pen, to be sure, not the metaphorical sword (Reagan's and George H. W.'s people).

But there is an irony in all this. It involves, not surprisingly, the two ways that those of the pen—in particular those of the media—have become involved in modern politics, corresponding to "issue" vs. "image." The point is that the language-focused bourgeoisie have professionally created the very conditions for the viability of George W. Bush's "message," even as they perhaps long for the only theoretically imagined yesteryear when politics was supposedly "issue"-dominated—and purportedly free from economic influence as well! Of course, "message" has always been part of our politics; even Mr. Lincoln strived to be "on message," at Gettysburg and elsewhere. Contemporary critics do not see that it is merely the way that "message" now emerges that heightens the crisis they may perceive: that "message" rears up and—like Her Majesty's white horse—embarrasses the processes of self-governance of the civics textbook.

Look at that textbook account of governance. There is a whole foundation of Enlightenment political theory that underlies the noblest political actions of the revolutionaries who created this country. American democracy was established in the eighteenth century as "the great experiment" in relation to a "talking" political process—like a "talking cure" of Freudian psychoanalysis. Language is the medium of politics in this order of democratic self-government derived from philosophical views of Lord Bacon and of John Locke. Such a governmental order is internally self-regulating, abstractly speaking, in the same way that Bacon laid out the self-regulating nature of natural science as a truth-seeking enterprise.

Everything depends on talk, talk, talk: from our Constitution to our legislative process to our administrative and legal systems to the workings of public-sphere political communication and its feedback in election results. The language of the Constitution licenses or authorizes Congress to debate and pass legislation, as well as to regulate its own internal workings. Members of the houses of Congress are elected, so there is a direct feedback (for the Senate, perfected by Constitutional amendment). Such legislation as Congress passes implies all kinds of administrative follow-through by an Executive branch, headed by the President, also an at least indirectly elected official (though not usually via the Supreme Court). And since the *Marbury v. Madison* case (1803), the Supreme Court and its lower federal courts have taken it upon themselves to create administrative meaning for Constitutional and statutory language as the means of regulating the workings of government. Even the concepts of the Constitution do not in practice mean anything until tested by the cycling of this process. It is language all the way down.

In theory, this is the deeply rooted, completely language-dependent governmental framework of our politics, despite gradual change in some of its specific forms. So we have expectations about the *rational deployment of expository language*: language that speaks to truth and falsity—to what is and what is not—and language of argument—the dialectic of debate about what is and what ought-to-be. We expect governmental processes in all branches and at all levels of our reticulated system to reach a closure of verbally achieved "judgment" and "persuasion" that results in some action.

Theoretically, government works verbally. Practically, we acknowledge the influence of financial and other extra-governmental *quia pro quibus* in aspects of government—we call much of it corruption—though people are always anxious about this corrupting factor. (The order of most-to-least unacceptable seems to run from judiciary to executive to legislative. Buy a judge: very, very bad. Buy a president/governor/mayor: rather bad. Buy a federal/state/city legislator: well, what do you expect?) But notwithstanding, the public expects a government of language-mavens; the *semblance* must always be maintained of verbal expertise and verbal fluidity. It's the very majesty of democratic government. (And note how many people in government are lawyers, expert language-users par excellence, and how many young people who say they want to go into politics see legal training and a law degree as a first step.)

Critical to the whole system is the legitimated renewal of government through the electoral process, the very mechanism of consent of those governed. Here is where "message" centrally and forcefully comes in. Lincoln himself certainly understood this, as have the administrations of his successors, though some have been more able than others to be "on message" in a winning way. Today, a politician—certainly, someone aspiring to the Presidency—has to present him- (or her-?) self in relation to how "message" politics works. As I said at the outset, a candidate with only issues, issues, issues will not cut it; this never has worked.

This is especially so in our current era of electoral self-government. Our process has become increasingly frank as a species of what is termed Hegelian "politics of recognition." Identities—demographics, for example—are mobilized to the exercise of power, for example electoral power. And in turn governmental process "recognizes" identities in allowing access to itself—like a presiding officer "recognizing" someone so as to allow him or her access to the speaking "floor"—and in allocating to various identities goods, services, resources, etc. Ever hear of the "angry white male?" Ever hear of the "soccer mom?" Ever hear of the "welfare queen?" These are identities, and can be cast as subjects or objects of political process—those appealed to, as well as those in respect of whom one is appealed to.

It is a kind of 14th Amendment collectivist politics of the electoral process. The post-Civil War 14th Amendment, adopted in 1868, among other provisions prevents any of the states from "deny[ing] to any person within its jurisdiction the equal protection of the laws." It has been an effective avenue of legal action in the struggles of categories of people for governmental recognition of who-and-what they are (or want to be).

Accordingly, the struggles of many in power to recognize them or *not* to recognize them as "equal[ly] protect[ed]" by this or that government practice are at the very heart of how this country now works. (Note the new reading this gives to the figure of blindfolded Justice!) Politics is a subtle process of inclusions and exclusions. Candidates and officials and legislative bodies and even courts selectively "recognize" categories of persons whose "equal protection" must be considered—by courting votes, by administering laws in certain ways, by passing laws or not, and by interpreting statute one way or another. Politicos call it "[someone's] constituencies"; their media advisors call it "[their] markets."

A president, like any elected person, is caught in the middle of such a politics of recognition. So especially is a President's "message." The Lockean government of, by, and for language may be an idealized, theoretical model of democracy in America. Yet none other than Lincoln, recall, made this his very "message." He wrapped himself and his war in it: "this is what we're fighting to preserve and sustain." The politics of recognition, by contrast, is the increasingly obtrusive reality that if all politics—court cases, regulatory and administrative processes, and most to the point electoral politics—is local, it can also be made to be personal. (In retrospect, the equity feminist slogan that "the personal is the political" was perhaps more descriptive than hortatory!)

The media are key here. They are the elaborate networks of communicational institutions that shape personal identities in public. They have long been central to how identity is brought together with political process. This, obviously, has both positive and negative sides: trying actively to shape certain communications while trying actively to suppress others. Especially today, through technical support of broadcast media for communicating "message" with great immediacy, political figures and those in their target "recognized" political markets rely upon communicated "message" as the glue bonding them together. Truly a "mediated" charisma. It is much as in multi-media "brand"-focused advertising for goods and services. The idea is to help people define themselves by structuring a significant portion of their identity-image, their "life style," around use or consumption, "brand" conferring value on identity-image: "I'm a Ford Bronco kind of guy!" This kind of politics makes of language a means to "message"-relevant image rather differently from the way it works as the medium of Baconian-Lockean talking-democracy. And here's where Dubya's *really tryin'*!"

Presidentiary Misspeakingfulness

It's not as though President Bush is unique in his presidential misspeaking. Far from it. There's lots of presidential misspeaking we could focus on in the cumulative record of modern politics alone. One can summon to memory Lyndon Johnson and Richard Nixon, caught by their own taping system in White House meetings. The tapes reveal them to be speaking a rather foul, informal, obscenity-laced register of the language sometimes laden with derogatory epithets for the identities of people then clamoring for recognition—whose very votes they courted.

At his inauguration on the Capitol steps, Warren G. Harding repeated the whopper, "normalcy," for standard register <u>normality</u>, invented for his 1920 anti-Wilsonian campaign slogan—and it stuck! ("Not notions and nostrums, but normalcy!")

Those old enough to remember President Eisenhower's news conferences will recall that he gave the rhetorical figure of *anacoluthon* a breathtaking run for its money—broken, stop-and-start, incoherent fragments of sentences stopping and never ending, just ceasing in mid-construction. I recall as a child being socialized in elementary school in the mid-1950s to *The New York Times*, observing with Mrs. McNulty their innovation in reporting, printing exact transcripts of Ike's news conferences, just as they were delivered: three words and an em-dash, four more and an em-dash, seven more, dash, three, dash. Like a Morse code of concept dots connected by dashes, the rhetorical periods frequently petered out and ceased, rather than coming to any conclusion. Here are a few extreme examples of this style of reply to reporters' questions:

> "Well, it wasn't on his desk yet. It was a report that had—well, he didn't know whether it was a report. It was a study—he had—as he had seen it—and it had been going back and forth—and they had been going at it for a long time. And it wasn't ready at this moment—at least, for publication—and its eventual destiny—he had forgotten the details." [9 February 1955 press conference]

> "[A]t the same time, if we limit ourselves to [military aid], then I would say we are—it was a self-defeating effort because we must—by—particularly by technical help and sometimes by helping in investments—let them develop their resources so they can have a better life." [23 January 1957 press conference]

> "He—and some of them he didn't like at all—He was a really—not only to my mind—a great man. He's one of my—certainly—one of my greatest friends that's not of my nationality." [15 January 1959 press conference]

What did this guy mean? Being a grandfatherly figure by that time, Mr. Eisenhower had the cuddly look of concerned befuddlement. But it was the 1950s, after all, and Ike had both won the war—the big one, WWII—and settled the Korean Conflict— the little one. He used his immense centrist popularity to counteract the worst right-wing and isolationist elements in his own party. So, except for the Adlai Stevenson "I-told-you-so"s, everyone gave the old gent a pass on his incoherence (except my Pop, who referred to him as "Blubberhead, Jr.," recalling Herbert Hoover, for him the nickname's prototype). Revisionist pop historians even now claim it was Eisenhower's cunningly strategic backing-and-filling in the face of an aggressive White House press corps.

Now, the current President is a particular specimen of language use, intriguing in many respects. People have been poking fun since "W" has emerged to national prominence, really, when the earlier Reagan and Bush administrations-in-exile gave him the go-ahead and pledged to come in from their corporate pastures. After taking office, the administration's presidential image-shapers were much disturbed by the ridiculing aftereffects of full frontal, uncosmetized interaction of the President with press and other outsiders. What could the "spin"-folk do with all those deer-in-the-headlights freeze-ups when the guy was asked a substantial question of fact? And worse was what followed: like scenes from Peter Sellers' brilliant film *Being There*, the pastiche of improvisational ready-mades that could have been delivered by Chauncey Gardiner (Chance The Gardener): "When you have your own money, it means you've got more money to spend." Or is it a repeat of Poppy Bush or of Ike himself:

> "And so, in my State of the—my State of the Union—or state—my speech to the nation—what-

ever you want to call it—speech to the nation—I
asked Americans to give 4,000 years—4,000 hours
over the next—the rest of your life—of service to
America."

(This, though, to an adoring, $5,000-a-photo fund-
raising audience in Old Greenwich, Connecticut on 9
April 2002, as reported by *The Times*' Elizabeth
Bumiller.)

When you're handed lemons, make lemonade.
A couple of shaky months after having been installed
in office, the Dubya White House has gone back to
the pre-Eisenhower practice of allowing the press to
quote only "official" versions of all of the President's
remarks, i.e., ones from which all the fun stuff has
been deleted. They have confined videotaping and
photographing of live appearances exclusively to trust-
worthy audiences and venues, from which, save for the
occasional reportorial leak (see above), only the carefully rehearsed sound-bite line or two have emerged.
After the terrorist bombings in 2001, when
Commander-in-Chief *gravitas* had to be mixed into
the "message," the cover of quasi-military censorship,
too, became convenient.

More recently, apparently desperate, they have
taken many pains with constructing back-drops with
the "message"-words printed so that camera operators
and photographers can hardly avoid including them in
a headshot. So in print and television shots,
"Corporate responsibility" floats all around Mr. Bush
as he makes his huffy and stern, supposedly newswor-
thy remarks on Wall Street that CEO and CFO fraud,

embezzlement, and "malfeance" would not—or at least would no-longer-for-the-time-being—be tolerated by this administration! "Recovery" in no-nonsense, solid-white, bold serif—rather than the Seal of the President of the United States—graces the front of the red-draped dais behind which is seated the blue-suited Mr. Bush at his Baylor University "Economic Forum" in August, 2002. It is as though the administration's "message" personnel no longer trust even the dutiful media to convey the "message"-relevant themes in presidential stories—much less the President himself! So the staff now includes them as feel-good indelible picture captions. They are visually sewing Dubya's "message" onto his image like pinning easy-to-forget gloves to a schoolchild's winter coat. Pinned "spin" that leaves your head spinning.

The Linguistic Substance of the Style

The raw verbal material that is Dubya, gathered to much amusement during the 2000 presidential campaign, in fact continues unabated, to judge from the rare candid recordings we only occasionally now overhear or read. What kinds of linguistic facts about Mr. Bush's speech does this verbal material reveal to us? I have taken a major collection of it made during his candidacy and in the first, transcriptionally unsanitized months of his Presidency, and have classified them according to the kind of "misspeakingfulness" that is in evidence. Here are the kinds of things I have found in the collection of instances.

First, noteworthy rarities. There are very few examples of the following:

Register Violations:
> "One of the interesting initiatives we've taken in Washington, D.C., is we've got these vampire-busting devices. A vampire is a—a cell deal you can plug in the wall to charge your cell phone."
> [Denver, 14 August 2001]

> "The budget caps were busted, mightily so."
> [Washington, D.C., 22 February 2001]

These are of a sparse, but regular occurrence, especially when the twin pulls of Connecticut vs. Texas jostle with each other in Mr. Bush's verbal delivery. Observe in the first how Mr. Bush slips from a formal, expository register, speaking of "interesting initiatives" to a kind of commercial descriptor, "vampire-bust[er]"—remember the anti-radar dashboard device called a "Fuzz Buster?"—to the truly substandard, "a cell deal," a.k.a. <u>a</u> <u>gadget</u> (and recall its hypertrophic cutesy—though masculine, still!—form, <u>dealie-bob[ber]</u>!).

Compare Eliza Doolittle, for whom, in *Pygmalion*, Shaw wrote a drawing-room scene of hilarious register shifts. Having observed, in perfect RP pronunciation, that her "aunt died of influenza: so they said," the others react sympathetically, so she continues: "But it's my belief <u>they</u> <u>done</u> <u>the</u> <u>old</u> <u>woman</u> <u>in</u>." And the floodgates of Cockney open. Who, moreover, can forget the Lerner & Lowe version at the Royal Ascot race? "Come on, Dover, <u>move</u> <u>yer</u> <u>bloomin'</u> <u>arse</u>!"

A second, truly rare occurrence in my corpus consists of the single example of:

Grammatical hypercorrection:
"I'm looking forward to having dinner <u>with</u> <u>he</u> <u>and</u> <u>Mrs.</u> <u>Blair</u> on Friday night." [Washington, D.C., 22 February 2001; first press conference, quoted by Mark Shields]

Now this is diagnostically interesting.

Hypercorrection is the use of "too much of a good thing." It comes about in this way. We are frequently ill at ease about whether or not we are saying only the "standard register" forms of our language, and are correctly avoiding use of the nonstandard ones. Situations of language use exert different amounts of subliminal pressure on us to edit our verbal usage toward standard register as we are producing it. In written language, we can go back over our forms and edit them; in speaking this is much more difficult. At that threshold of semi-consciousness that is the editing function in speaking, the central fact is that there are alternatives one of which, the standard, is more highly valued than the other, the nonstandard. Sometimes we put in what *would be* the standard form in a different, but related grammatical construction— but not in the particular construction we are using— because we are so nervously focused on the fact that valued standard and de-valued nonstandard forms coexist: "*Whom* shall I say is calling?" (In standard register, <u>who</u> ought to be marked as the grammatical subject form for the predicate phrase <u>is</u> <u>calling</u>, of course; the higher clause <u>shall</u> <u>I</u> <u>say</u> takes the whole lower clause as its object. In contemporary English spoken vernacular we simply collapse the semantic distinction between the forms <u>who</u> and <u>whom</u> in favor of using <u>who</u> at the beginning of a clause. So use of <u>whom</u> has cachet as the high-falootin' form—if you can use it according to its older semantic rule! Which, of course, you don't when you hypercorrect.)

"Just between you and *I*..." (In written standard, the phrase <u>you</u> <u>and</u> <u>me</u> is the object of the preposition <u>between</u>, so both pronouns, <u>you</u> and <u>me</u>, are marked for that grammatical function. Vernacular spoken English uses the <u>me</u> form, however, when the pronoun bears stress or is final in its phrase. So, anxiously avoiding the stereotypically déclassé—and impolite—<u>me</u> <u>and</u> <u>him</u>, as in "Me 'n' him wen' t' da game," hypercorrect use of I becomes an index of distinction, even after the preposition.)

    …—and so forth. Observe in each case the existence of at least one anxiety-causing explicit rule dearly loved of standard-register grammar teachers. So the nonvernacular alternant becomes endowed with that *soupçon* of distinction-conferring value. And so long as one has internalized *the grammatical conditions under which actual speakers of standard use it*, fine. But there is pressure to use it whenever one or the other form of the set should occur—whom (even where use of who would be standard), I (even for me). So people do.

    Now hypercorrection is usually evidence of demonstrable linguistic insecurity, a degree of unease about our own and about others' standard usage that comes from our anxiety about norms. Such anxiety is apparently unequally distributed across society. It shows up again and again in various studies of what is termed the sociolinguistic stratification of a language community. This is a picture of the way that differences in a society's language use—the pronunciation, grammar, vocabulary, what-have-you that people use on occasions of communication—correlate with differences in people's societal position. For example, when we look at the different rates at which, under various conditions, different kinds of people in society produce, or attempt to produce, "standard" forms, we get a picture of the sociolinguistic stratification of their language. The studies of William Labov and others reveal interesting characteristics in this respect for aspects of language subject to such anxieties.

Labov and others select a form that has wide variation in a language community that seems to be a function of speaker demographics and attitudes. They create scales to count and measure the degree of "standardness" (rate of using a standard form) vs. "nonstandardness" (rates of various nonstandard alternants) of language-production by people of known demographic characteristics under different, specifiable conditions of usage.

Look at one typical result for an aspect of language that is subject to standard-anxiety. We find that the rates at which people perform "standard" do, in fact, vary. The accompanying Figure 4 is taken from William Labov's early 1960s studies of New York City English on the Lower East Side of Manhattan (before gentrification). It shows the pronunciation of <r> at the end of syllables, as in words written "partner," "shore," etc. by speakers of various socioeconomic classes under different conditions of speaking. These conditions run from overheard private conversation with a familiar, up through the task of reading target words aloud from a printed page for the interviewer. Observe how the hyper-anxious "lower middle class" speakers hypercorrect way beyond the rate of production of post-vocalic [r] pronunciations even of the "upper middle class" speakers, whose language, more or less invariant across these task demands, is relatively like standard. (They do pronounce <r> consistently most of the time.) The hypercorrecters are saying things like "[laryer]" for the word lawyer, "[sowfer]" for the word sofa, and so on. They're so anxious about dropping the <r>s where they should be

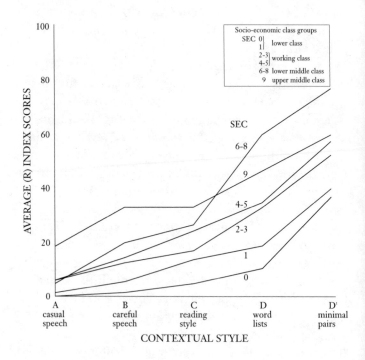

Figure 4.

putting them in, that they overshoot what plausibly seems to be the target, the prestige form of speech of the standard register.

When people are basically non-standard speakers, and are anxious about it, as soon as some speaking situation arises in which standard would be demanded, or even expected, they start moving abruptly away from their basically non-standard patterns of speech toward the standard. And beyond. I believe that in our evidence, at the level of standard grammar, Mr. Bush reveals himself to be basically secure in his use of English as a grammatical system—though it would be interesting to see if he has been made less so by the comic barrage of Bushism-bashing. He is emphatically *not* one of the anxious, "chattering classes," as people like professors and lawyers and reporters and such would be termed, all people who make a living by using language expertly. And he's *certainly not* of the lower middle class, where, characteristically, linguistic insecurity and hypercorrection cluster together!

So Mr. Bush appears to be relatively outside of that system of anxieties. Or *is* he? We might view his usage against the backdrop of expectably coherent expository prose—"U. S. Government Jeffersonian and Madisonian standard," we might term it. What kinds of violations against good textual sense does Mr. Bush's usage demonstrate? I have classified the other kinds of Mr. Bush's verbal nonstandards, abundantly in evidence in the collection (though some examples show more than one dimension of unacceptability as standard discourse). These types are:

Incoherence by locution:

Here, a sentence that starts off with one syntactic form and word-choice veers off into semantic incoherence when a conflicting construction or contradictory word-choice shapes the talk later in the flow. At least we think it's incoherence: sometimes, as these examples show, W seems inadvertently to be speaking from a subliminal font of truth!

> "My administration has been calling upon all the leaders in the—in the Middle East to do everything they can <u>to</u> <u>stop</u> <u>the</u> <u>violence</u>, to tell the different parties involved that <u>peace</u> <u>will</u> <u>never</u> <u>happen</u>."
> [Crawford, TX, 13 August 2001]

If one "stop[s] the violence," that is usually called a state of "peace," of course. But if one is fighting for peace—and aren't we all?—maybe it *will* never happen!

> "I haven't <u>had</u> <u>a</u> <u>chance</u> <u>to</u> <u>talk</u>, but I'm confident we'll get a bill that I can live with <u>if</u> <u>we</u> <u>don't</u>."
> [Brussels, 13 June 2001]

Perhaps the suggestion here was to be that *even if* Mr. Bush could not confer, an acceptable bill would emerge from the legislative process—or maybe no bill at all. What he instead suggests—no doubt echoing Messrs. Daschle and Gephardt, and perhaps Messrs. Cheney and Rumsfeld as well—is that he should specifically keep his hands off that process!

"For every fatal shooting, there were <u>roughly</u> three non-fatal <u>shootings</u>. And, folks, <u>this</u> is unacceptable in America. <u>It's</u> just unacceptable. And we're going to <u>do</u> <u>something</u> <u>about</u> <u>it</u>." [Philadelphia, 14 May 2001]

Dubya must think that the 1:3 ratio of fatal to nonfatal shootings must be increased, from the way he phrased this! Perhaps it's the "take-no-patients" approach of his federal healthcare policies toward hospital emergency rooms.

"First, we would <u>not</u> <u>accept</u> a treaty that would <u>not</u> <u>have</u> <u>been</u> <u>ratified</u>, <u>nor</u> a treaty that I thought <u>made</u> <u>sense</u> for the country." [*Washington Post*, 24 April 2001]

Could The President, having put in so many negatives in the first several phrases, gotten "negative exhaustion" where it really counted, making sense for the country?

"We're concerned about AIDS <u>inside</u> <u>our</u> <u>White</u> <u>House</u>—make no mistake about it!" [Washington, D.C., 7 February 2001]

Does Mr. Bush harbor suspicions about somebody's secret history of unprotected political or financial practices? Even after the Clinton administration?

"I mean there needs to be <u>a</u> <u>wholesale</u> <u>effort</u> against racial profiling, <u>which</u> <u>is</u> <u>illiterate</u> <u>children</u>." [2nd Presidential Debate, 11 October 2000].

Can this wholesale effort really reach its goal of illiteracy for all of our children?

> "I understand <u>small</u> <u>business</u> growth; I <u>was</u> <u>one</u>."
> [*New York Daily News*, 19 February 2000]

Perhaps the speaker wishes candidly to indicate that as a young man he *was* a small, if somewhat benign and ineffectual, growth on business; then again, given insider-trading scandals, perhaps he does not.

> "This administration is doing everything we can to end the stalemate in an efficient way. We're making the right decisions <u>to</u> <u>bring</u> <u>the</u> <u>solution</u> <u>to</u> <u>an</u> <u>end</u>."
> [Washington, D.C., 10 April 2001]

Ending solutions, as for example to global warming, to toxic dump-site cleanup, to separation of church and state, to yearly budget surpluses, and so forth, certainly has been a hallmark of the younger Bush administration.

Verbose redundancies/incoherence:

Here is classic "double-talk:" precise or near synonyms are strung together so as only to seem to be making an informative statement about some topic. Through this device, one adds maximal verbiage and minimal—if any—new (denotational) thought.

> "I knew it might put him in an awkward position *that* we had a discussion <u>before</u> <u>finality</u> <u>has</u> <u>finally</u> <u>happened</u> in this presidential race." (*nonstandard grammar for:* if) [Crawford, TX, 2 December 2000]

Finality, of course, has a propensity to happen finally, especially when closure is reached.

"It's very important for folks to understand that when there's <u>more trade</u>, there's <u>more commerce</u>." [Quebec City, 21 April 2001]

One wonders if there's also more business, more pecuniary activity, etc.?

"Redefining the role of the United States from *enablers to* <u>keep the peace</u> to *enablers to* <u>keep the peace from peacekeepers</u> is going to be an assignment." (*broken grammar*, too) [*New York Times* interview, 14 January 2001]

It must, of course, be a very tricky assignment "to keep the peace from peacekeepers," must it not? But surely we must commend the then President-elect's continuing his resolve to do something about all that peace being kept around the world, especially by peacekeepers enabled by the previous administration.

"The California crunch is really the result of <u>not enough power-generating plants</u> and then <u>not enough power to power the power of generating plants</u>." [*New York Times* interview, 14 January 2001]

What powers of powers be these of which ye speak, My Liege? The nth power: the power of the Texas firm Enron to drain Democratic Governor Gray Davis' state treasury of some 50 billions of its surplus dollars while the federal regulators under Mr. Bush "helplessly" watched?

"I'm hopeful. I know there is a lot of <u>ambition</u> in Washington, obviously. But I hope <u>the ambitious</u> realize that they are more likely <u>to succeed with success</u> as opposed to <u>failure</u>." [Associated Press interview, 18 January 2001]

This must be a clever rewording, must it not, of the administration's bromide for business people, "Do as I say, not as I did!" Those others in Washington ambitious "to succeed with failure" certainly were discouraged from government service when the administration took over.

"<u>Home is important. It's important to have a home</u>." [Crawford, TX, 18 February 2001]

You can say that again! And root, root, root for the "home" team!

"Our nation must <u>come together</u> to <u>unite</u>." [Tampa, FL, 4 June 2001]

No two ways about it, for sure! Divided unity can be, at best, half-baked.

"I know <u>what I believe</u>. I will continue to articulate <u>what I believe</u> and <u>what I believe</u>—<u>I believe what I believe</u> is right." [Rome, 22 July 2001]

It is good that Mr. Bush explained so forcefully to the European audience just whose beliefs about his beliefs about his beliefs about…—whatever they actually consist of!—are "right!"

Broken grammar (anacoluthon with/without repair):

An utterance starts off as one construction type, and then, with or without a hesitation or break in the talk, it continues as though it were a very different construction type. Sometimes the speaker goes back to start up again from a prior position that allows the transition to the new grammatical form.

> "The fact that he *relies on facts—says things that are not factual—*are going to undermine his campaign." (*incoherence*, too) [*New York Times*, 4 March 2000]

Starting out to say that a certain fact *is* going to undermine Mr. Gore's campaign, at mid-sentence, when "he relies on facts" is incoherently glossed as "[he] says things that are not factual"—there's a "lie" in "rely," after all!—those "things that are not factual" become the subject of the—now correct—"*are* going...." Of course, Mr. Gore *was* plagued in his campaign by both "facts:" that he relied pedantically on "facts, facts, facts," at the very same time that Mr. Bush's people relentlessly accused him of saying "non-factual" things.

> "The person who runs FEMA [Federal Emergency Management Administration] is someone who must have the trust of the President. Because the person who runs FEMA is the first voice, often times,—of—someone whose life has been turned upside down—hears—from." [Austin, TX, 4 January 2001]

The poor guy seems to be trying to express the complex thought that [1] a natural-disaster victim, "someone whose life has been turned upside down," *hears* the voice of FEMA first, perhaps even that of "the person who runs FEMA," and that [2] the President *hears from* the FEMA director first and so must trust that person. All of these constructions, plus the nonsensical "the person who runs FEMA is the first voice…of…someone whose life has been turned upside down" are woven together, turned upside down, in an unmanageable syntactic disaster of enormous proportion.

> "So <u>on</u> <u>behalf</u> <u>of</u>—<u>a</u> **well-oiled** **unit** <u>of</u> <u>people</u> who came together to serve something greater than *themselves*—<u>congratulations</u>!" (**register-shift**, *nonstandard grammar*) [Washington, D.C., 31 May 2001 (U of Nebraska women's volleyball team, national champions 2001)]

Well, getting "well-oiled" might not at first seem to be the way to "serve" in volleyball, but Dubya should know; he is reputed to have been well oiled throughout his youth. Here he seems to be having a great deal of difficulty discerning on behalf of whom he's serving up congratulations—or is the White House team, too, "well-oiled?" (As for the other virtue, we certainly know that, among others, Mr. Ashcroft professes to "serve something greater than [himself]!")

> "*There's a lot* of people in the Middle East who are desirous to get into the Mitchell process. <u>And</u>—<u>but</u> first things first. <u>The</u>—<u>these</u> terrorist acts and, you know, the responses, have got to end in order for us

to get <u>the</u> <u>framework</u>—<u>the</u> <u>groundwork</u>—<u>not</u> <u>the</u> <u>framework</u>—<u>the</u> <u>groundwork</u> to discuss a framework for peace—<u>to</u> <u>lay</u> <u>the</u>—<u>all</u> <u>right</u>." (*substandard grammar*, too) [Crawford, TX 13 August 2001]

All right! Beyond the hesitant self-corrections at the beginning, Mr. Bush finally gets to the presumably diplomatic formula he must dimly remember from a briefing or ten, "groundwork to discuss a framework for peace" in the Israeli-Palestinian conflict. But he recalled only the nominal part, and forgot that "groundworks" are "laid," in the idiom. So he tacks it on at the end, like a reverse-order index entry. Completed, sort 'a. Whew!

"If <u>he's</u>—<u>the</u> <u>inference</u> <u>is</u> that somehow he thinks slavery <u>is</u> <u>a</u>—<u>is</u> <u>a</u>—noble institution <u>I</u> <u>would</u>—<u>I</u> <u>would</u>—strongly reject <u>that</u> <u>assumption</u>—<u>that</u> John Ashcroft is a[*] open-minded, inclusive person." [*NBC Nightly News*, 14 January 2001]

This utterance itself is so inclusive, it winds up hinting at a war among Dubya's head, heart, and deep-seated heart-of-hearts. If in his heart-of-hearts the President rejects the "assumption…that John Ashcroft is a[n] open-minded, inclusive person," maybe he has given reason to others so to "infer"—and worse, as the first claim reports. Another one where too much is going on for the speaker to keep track of—who's on first, what's on second, and so forth, semantically speaking.

Broken grammar (non-standard and substandard):

Even with no indication of the stop-and-start of anacoluthon (though this sometimes accompanies), fluent but grammatically ill-formed sentences occur. The corpus is full of the predictably substandard usage (charitably to be interpreted as dialectal?) that grammar and diction teachers have long and fruitlessly been inveighing against in elementary grades. Subject-verb agreement, for example, seems to be a major stumbling block for Mr. Bush.

"She is a member of a labor union <u>at</u> <u>one</u> <u>point</u>." [Austin, TX, 2 January 2001]

Is this like being joined (as a member) at the hip? At least a past tense form, "was a member," would have helped this dangler.

"Of all <u>states</u> that <u>understands</u> local control of schools, Iowa is such a state." [Council Bluffs, IA, 28 February 2001]

"But the true <u>greatness</u> of America <u>are</u> the people." [Jefferson Memorial, Washington, D.C., 2 July 2001]

"Our <u>priorities</u> <u>is</u> our faith." [Greensboro, NC, 10 October 2000]

"Laura and I really don't realize how bright <u>our</u> <u>children</u> <u>is</u> sometimes until we get an objective analysis." [CNBC, 15 April 2000]

Singular or plural, we still understands what the man mean, don't we?

> "We understand where the power of this country *lay*. It <u>lays</u> in the hearts and souls of Americans. It must <u>lay</u> in our pocketbooks. It <u>lays</u> in the <u>willingness</u> <u>for</u> people to work hard. But as importantly, it <u>lays</u> in the fact that we've got citizens from all walks of life, all political parties, that are willing to say, I want to love my neighbor." (*ungrammatical*, too) [Concord, NC, 11 April 2001]

—or is that "I want to lay my neighbor?" Well, there's loving and there's loving, after all! As can be seen, this is not a random slip; it's that old teachers' bugaboo, (to) *lie* (down) ["intransitive"] versus (to) *lay* (something down) ["transitive"]. (And then there were the pasts, *lay* and *laid*, and those suggestive participles to torture us, *lain* and *laid*! What's a [Good Ol'] boy to do?) Perhaps Mr. Bush just had "Lay"—as in Kenny Boy—or DeLay—as in Tom—too much on his mind!

> "I have said that the <u>sanction</u> <u>regime</u> is like Swiss cheese—that meant that <u>they</u> weren't very effective." [Washington, D.C., 22 February 2001]

> "Whatever it took to help <u>Taiwan</u> defend <u>theirself</u>." [*Good Morning America!* 25 April 2001]

> "You teach <u>a</u> <u>child</u> to read, and <u>he</u> <u>or</u> <u>her</u> will be able to pass a literacy test." [Townsend, TN, 21 February 2001]

So not only agreement of verbs and their subjects, but as well agreement of anaphoric pronouns and their antecedents, are full of holes in W's usage. Or just substandard. The last one is touching, of course, since it shows what happens when the President attempts gender-neutral anaphoric usage, as prescribed by all those bra-burning feminists. Finally, the poetry of a grammatical spoonerism added to a grammatical mismatch:

> "<u>Families</u> <u>is</u> where our nation finds hope, where *wings take dream.*" [La Crosse, WI, 18 October 2000]

Ignorance of terms, morphology, and referents:
Here we find a plethora of coinages akin to Mr. Harding's. A misspeakingful creation substitutes for a perfectly ordinary, expectable term we can almost guess from context. We also find that Mr. Bush uses particular words in senses wildly different, if not opposite to the norm. Especially do we find use of expressions indicating the speaker has—at least temporarily—no real idea as to what these terms pick out in the world.

> "I do think *we need for* <u>a</u> <u>troop</u> to be able to house <u>his</u> family. That's an important part of building morale in the military." (*substandard grammar*, too) [Tyndall Air Force Base, FL, 12 March 2001]

Given this charming concoction, we might conclude that Mr. Bush speaks of each vertical half of his trousers as <u>a</u> <u>pant</u>, or as well of one part of a cutting instrument as <u>a</u> <u>scissor</u>!

"Well, I think that if you say you're going to do
something and don't do it, that's trustworthiness."
[*CNN Online Chat*, 30 August 2000]

And here I thought it was misspeakingfulness!
Note that, increasingly, many people have accused the
Bush administration of using Orwellian Newspeak;
perhaps more folks should have been alerted by such
early indications of upside-down semantics during his
candidacy.

"It's going to require numerous IRA agents." ("it" =
Al Gore's tax plan) [Greensboro, NC, 10 October
2000]

This gives a whole new sense to getting one's
Irish up! IRS—INS—IRA; who can keep them all
straight? Dick? John? Don? Are you there? Which
bunch is in charge of my "War on Terror?"

"Neither in French nor in English nor in
Mexican." [Quebec City, 21 April 2001]

Don't we have a NAF TA do to try to speak
just *one* of the major North American languages? This
gaffe was worthy of Dan Quayle, who thought the
"Latin Americans" must be speaking in "Latin!"

"They want the federal government controlling
Social Security like it's some kind of federal program." [St. Charles, MO, 2 November 2000]

Looking forward to the day that his privatization plan for Social Security accounts would get Congressional approval, candidate W must already have been subliminally imagining what Arthur Andersen & Co. could do to re-balance the budget!

> "There are some monuments where the land is <u>so</u> <u>widespread, they just encompass as much as possible</u>. And the <u>integral</u> part of the—the <u>precious</u> part, so to speak—I guess all land is precious—but the part that people uniformly would not want to <u>spoil</u>, will not be <u>despoiled</u>." (several anacolutha, too) [Washington, D.C., 13 March 2001]

The difficulties with diction here are monumental, to be sure! So much so, they seem to have spoiled, or perhaps even despoiled, the integral and precious thought encompassed.

Finally, lurching ever more definitively into the abyss of diction and grammar beyond the President's ken, we come to the Bushisms that have proven the most fun for *Saturday Night Live* and *The Capitol Steps* and fun-pokers on the Internet:

(Classic) Malapropisms:

George Bush is the best thing since Mrs. Malaprop herself!

> "Ann [Veneman] and I will <u>carry out</u> this <u>equivocal</u> message to the world: markets must be open!" [Washington, D.C., 2 March 2001]

In fact, markets must *unequivocally* be open! That is no doubt why dead, equivocal messages have to be carried out to the trash-heap of history.

> "A tax-cut is really one of the <u>anecdotes</u> <u>to</u> coming out of an economic illness." [*The Edge* with Paula Zahn, 18 September 2000]

But boy, it really packs a wallop on such infections as Treasury surpluses! And have you heard the one about the last time a President had trickle-down disease?

> "And we need <u>a</u> <u>full</u> <u>affront</u> <u>on</u> an energy crisis that is real in California and looms for other parts of our country if we don't move quickly." [Washington, D.C., 29 March 2001]

And here we thought that Enron's CEO and Mr. Cheney's Energy Task Force worked as fast as they could to assault California's state treasury as well as other parts of the country with a full affrontal plan!

> "What I am against is quotas. I am against hard quotas; quotas, they basically <u>delineate</u> based upon whatever. However they <u>delineate</u>, quotas, I think, <u>vulcanize</u> society." [*San Francisco Chronicle*, 21 January 2000]

My understanding was that only *elastic* quotas need "vulcaniz[ing]," however. And I certainly draw the line at delineation, as should everyone!

"Anyway, I'm so thankful, and so <u>gracious</u>. I'm <u>gra-cious</u> that my brother Jeb is concerned about the hemisphere as well." [Miami, 4 June 2001]

Even though "gracious," one should, I guess, not be shy about it!

"You <u>subscribe</u> politics to it. I <u>subscribe</u> freedom to it." ("it" = the Elián González affair) [Associated Press quote, 6 April 2000]

This must depend on what magazine ascriptions you're signed up for, I imagine. Poor guy; he must have gotten miscued somewhere along the speech process by talking to the Associated *Press*—you know, the people who publish those things you "*subscribe to!*"

The Collage and Montage of "Message"

As I noted, the "message" professionals in the current White House are concerned enough to have made great efforts at controlling public access to Dubya's spontaneous speech. Yet, in spite of problems it has when measured against fluid, fluent, spoken expository standard speech, there are important, "message"-worthy aspects of it. Aspects that the public and the media have responded to quite positively. And since the air-borne terrorist attacks of September 11, 2001, Mr. Bush's image has been almost exclusively narrowed to the embodied message of strength and seriousness—Texas-bred [!] toughness—in "really trying" to cope with "evil" and to succeed at doing so beyond (others') expectations. To this, there has been positive reaction even from *The New York Times*.

Others around him—his top Cabinet members, his top staff members—appear in the media sounding informed, professional, and on top of things; they sound off in expository standard English. Where media appearances have been arranged for him, Mr. Bush is shown projecting a determination to cope and win—with all of his being, it seems, as he makes a hard, breathy attack on every consonant of every important syllable he speaks, dysfluent as it may be when left unscripted. It's plosive-pounding punches from the jaw of determination, folks.

Miraculously rescued miners in Pennsylvania in summer, 2002: a case in point. Here was an opportunity to show that this rescue effort had coped with the crisis and succeeded against the odds. Both the personnel above ground and the trapped miners below, using all their ingenuity, had "really tried." So a media ritual occasion was duly arranged to show that it's the same with terrorism, of which the "message"-opportunity for W would make the rescue a metaphor. Not, note, an occasion for dramatizing the issue of mine-shaft safety (Too pro-labor and anti-company? Too associated with Democrats?), or even the soothing, pro-status-quo and pro-business reassurance that a safety-net exists even for miners terrorized below terra firma. The denotational nonsequitur is unimportant; the moment of Vygotskian chain-conceptualization is all. The fluency or dysfluency of the language of W's remarks is unimportant; what carries is the rich visual context of the event's crafting: the President dressed to look like a miner, standing at the same level and in a group with them, breaking into jocular, congratulatory holds, pats on the shoulder, etc. Not victims, but survivors. In-and-by surviving, not merely rescued men, but burly quasi-heroes. The President forcefully articulates in his no-nonsense syllabary style the now metonymic as well as metaphoric comparison-words in which "America" coming to the "rescue" of "freedom" from terrorism stands tall with the rescuers/rescued. We get the picture.

That's how and why this particular kind of political "message" language works. It is the culminative coming together of a politics of recognition—a two-way affair with a public that encompasses a politician's electorate—with a very contemporary sensibility about language and its power to contribute to image. Language reformed for a *People Magazine* politics.

To be sure this is not Lincoln's sensibility about "message" language, though in moments of serious crisis every President, including George Bush, has had to make some stab at Lincolnesque preacherliness, with its evangelist-like affective loading. Mr. Bush, for example, did just fine with the register in the course of three formal speeches crafted for his delivery in mid-September, 2001; each had moments of resonance with the canon in what we can term the Lincoln-derived "civil religious register."

Yet, consider the one-year commemoration of the terrorist attacks, on September 11, 2002. Officialdom, in the respectful silence of things-still-beyond-them, turned again to the very thing, Lincoln's Gettysburg Address. It was proclaimed over "Ground Zero" in New York City, thereby consecrating it as "hallowed ground" in the longer sweep of American sacred nationhood. The dead firefighters, police, and even office and restaurant workers all become construable as heroes for the administration's current "unfinished work" against terrorism. Even at the Pentagon that day, another site of damage a year earlier, Lincoln's words "these dead shall not have died in vain" needed to be used for properly honoring, thus also assimilating, the dead of the Department of Defense. Only immortal Lincoln can *really* "cope" when the rhetorical task before us is this great. Lincoln's text has, indeed, proved to be of a truly transcendent "message"-worthiness. (But consider this.

Shanksville, Pennsylvania was the crashsite of the truly heroic citizens on board American Airlines flight 93. On September 11th, no one recycled Lincoln's rhetoric at the commemoration there, an out-of-the-way and starkly less monumental site. Ironically enough, the visuals of the site compare with the starkness of Cemetery Hill outside Gettysburg in 1863 where the rhetoric itself made the site monumental.)

So when the going gets tough, the tough get Lincoln. But what about in between such Lincoln-worthy moments? Talking politics is publicly experienced nowadays through a very different, this-worldly rhetorical sensibility. It rests upon a different set of intertextual connections, to what I would term *corporatized language*. Fashioned along the lines of modern advertising copy, language in this mode is very precisely composed by phrases and words as the units, not by sentences and paragraph-chunks of denotational exposition. It's a compositional "language"—really, a code—of imagery. It uses what look and sound like words, but ideally, each contributory word or expression counts as a kind of autonomous emblem of an identity, targeting the sensibilities of a position in social reality. Someone is out there, at this or that number in a demographic scale; leaning this or that way in an attitudinal profile scale; etc. The potential is for such an emblem to "speak" to a targeted type of addressee, whom it invites to identify with a product, a service, a person, a corporation, a goal—whatever is being marketed. Flash the composite text of all the right emblems, and you get the keys to the kingdom.

It's the *Language,* Stupid!

Not unrelated to this contemporary development in political language is the following history. In 1976 (and years following) the U.S. Supreme Court brought commercial speech under a particular kind of First Amendment protection. This is popularly coded as protection of "free speech." The Court was almost droll in its legal construal of advertising. It took it to be purposive communication of truths about a product, etc. under consideration for purchase, etc. by the addressee, the potential buyer. In this way, an advertisement's text is seen as expository prose, even if frequently somewhat distorted by overblown claims (termed "puffery") about one's wares. Expository prose that ought to be protected—not "abridged"—when considered as generally honest, sincere communication of important messages in the ordinary sense of the term.

Observe, however, what follows as a consequence for the now "protected" legal realm of advertising content: it could be scrutinized for accurate (or inaccurate) propositional statements explicitly made or conventionally "implicated"—that is, suggested to the ordinary citizen-addressee by what was explicitly claimed. And this, obviously, exposes advertising copy to regulation and to lawsuit as truthful communication. Think of the disgruntled customers who think they were misled by propositional content. Think of suspicious regulatory overhearers of such communication, as for example the FDA testing claims made by purveyors of quack as well as of legit medical products.

Since the late 1970s, as Richard Parmentier points out in a study of regulation and "puffery," advertisers' textual use of direct and propositionally complete factual generalizations about the goods and services advertised has plummeted. Who wants to be taken to have made a cause-and-effect statement these days? Remember "99 and 44/100ths % pure. So pure…it floats?" (The soap turned out to float because each bar, made of whipped ("puffed?") sodium stearate and other stuff, had a very high air content. Three dots as printed were not enough to prevent Jane Doe from being misled and understanding "unintended" cause and effect relations here.)

Instead, advertising copy in the public realm concentrates much more on the selection and artful textual organization of images and of detachable words and phrases, static or dynamic as the particular medium allows. In text and image, it may narrate stories about characters, even purportedly "real" people, as a mode of "third-person" testimonial. But when we look for expository claims directly about the marketable thing itself, we find instead a high number of denotationally incomplete sentences and sentence fragments, registered slogans and catch-words, and other—as we may term it—residually poetic material, grammatically problematic but artistically put together. One frequently encounters specific claims, but they will be claims about "you"—or a stand-in, an "image-you" the real you is supposed to project onto. These claims will be about how "you" feel, think, or desire, or how "you" ought to be having some other reaction that causes anxiety relative to sometimes not so subtle norms in the product's market sphere. (Think cosmetics and looking-one's-age anxieties. Think certain automobiles and parents' child-safety anxieties. Think more-or-less anything and sex.)

Why should this be? It is a strategic retreat, to be sure, from what the Supreme Court declared to be the expository or informational value of commercial communication. But the retreat is one perfectly consistent with how politics in public now moves far away from language as the instrument of precise articulation of "issues" the public can experience via politicians' truth-claims and especially—Poppy, are you listening?—promises. In fact, the politics of recognition has ultimately found its very semiotic technology of "message," a technology whose expert practitioners are verbal, visual, and media artists of sometimes great accomplishment. With its history of slogans, catchwords, and multi-modal orchestration of "message"—Gettysburg was no exception, recall—American politics long has provided the raw materials for their artistic labor. Now it provides major and continuing employment, most effectively, it seems, by the RNC. (It was advertising bigwigs who, "liking Ike," came to General Eisenhower to persuade him in effect to leave the 1952 campaign to them.)

In the current state of the "message" art, moreover, all of the other institutions of political life, and especially the public, have seemed to adjust. We see and hear political communication with the eyes and ears of consumers of "message." Even news sources now duly package politicians for use along these lines. They just accept "message" as what is at issue in political life. And continuing stories give politicians biographical continuity in relation to "message." Insiders' connoisseurship of the product, as it were. One's biography *is*—or *becomes*—one's "message," remember.

(Interestingly, the "messages" of the "major brands" themselves, Republican and Democratic, may well have become too compromised as such for the electorate and the public-at-large. Yet at least for an electoral cycle the apparatus of either party "brand" can be put at the disposal of a politician who can define his or her independent "message"—frequently a "message" (brand) with a strong anti-"brand" stance! Recall Mr. Reagan the "outsider" to Washington politics, and young Bush in his image. The parallel to market forces in fashion and taste is not at all fortuitous, since it operates with much the same logic. Seen always and only as a potentially "brand"able image, any initially counter-cultural emergent can be assimilated to the larger system of commodity-value so that its "message" *now within* the system is "I'm not in the [= those other folks'] system," e.g., punk or "Goth" clothing, hip-hop music, etc. Remember the 7-Up ad campaign in which this brand took upon itself the soubriquet "The Un-cola," aimed principally at the Pepsi- and Coca-Cola generation thirsting to break free.)

But here is the most telling fact. There is a reciprocal effect, too. It is exerted on the very nature and meaningfulness of language as the stuff, the medium, of communication in the public sphere. The effect is seen in an adjustment of the ratio of operative meanings in any linguistic expression, the denotational and the context-indicating. Both are always present, always involved in communication. But think of any words or expressions that have been finely ground through the mill of "message"-copy. These words and expressions are particularly precise in suggestively communicating the identity "who" and the contextual "why" of their use. Not necessarily much in the way of precise denotation. "Hey, where's the beef?"—"Make my day!"—"I like Ike!"—"…whom you trust…"—…. The more of these that constitute the currency of our mutual adjustments one to another, the more these kinds of words and expressions imperceptibly influence the way we listen for them as a shortcut to understanding the world: thus, "…freedom…"— "…peace…"—"…honor…" in the texts of political "message." The key expressions are no longer experienced—or *to be experienced*—as signals of concepts with which we communicate denotational truth-and-falsity. As we encounter them in circulation, they are doing their work of socially locating speakers and addressees, and reinforcing their emblematic power to do such work. Their potency lies in how they conjure up a kind-of-"who" at a certain cultural "where." And of course this is precisely what is central to building "message" through carefully—artfully—fashioned exposure designed for such purposes.

But this is exactly how language itself—and in particular what we might term "corporate standard register"—is actually being marketed. The addressees

are aspiring people who are uncertain about their fit-
ness to join the ranks of middle management and
higher. So language is being authoritatively marketed
as indexical Viagra for the yupwardly mobile, essen-
tially in pill or pellet form. And complete with size-
anxiety: "Success in your business or profession and
the size of your vocabulary show a definite correla-
tion," Learn, Inc.'s Vocabulary Program advertise-
ments inform the underendowed. (And you can self-
administer the remedies in the privacy of your own
home. Forget the embarrassment of English—let
alone gym—class!)

So what is going on is the quantization of language, standard-sized packaging. We get a language
being turned word-by-word and grammatical-con-
struction-by-grammatical-construction into a collection of life-style commodities. Available to the cus-
tomer or client for self-help. "Acquire a powerful
vocabulary that catapults you into the top 5% of all
educated adults—the most successful, highest-earning
people!" screams the ad for "Verbal Advantage®
Success Edition" vocabulary audiocassettes. "Put a $ in
front of each word you learn," as you move up the
corporate ladder, circulate in the best clubs, and pick
up the most desirable partners.

It's language broken down into a word-by-
word display of one's target identity, words to throw
into one's speech for impression-management. There
is indeed an anxiety that creates the market; it is the
anxiety of the would-be Harvard M.B.A.—maybe
would-be President!—who lives in the world of indexical meaning, whose experience of language, whose

sense of what language is about, is the world of indexical meaning. "Paradigm—Transcend—Discursive—Ubiquitous—Stratagem:" "Do you know these words? … Can you use them… with confidence and accuracy?" asks the brochure for Career Success Vocabulary Cassettes, available only through American Express. "Now, you can amass a Harvard graduate's vocabulary in just 15 minutes a day!" Verbal Advantage® reassures us. Our current Harvard M.B.A. Chief Magistrate and Commander-in-Chief is living proof.

Real-"message"-Politik

In a very real sense, then, there has emerged an agreement, an implicit contract between politicians and the vast pool of media to use the "axis of 'message'" to mediate the relationship of political figures and the public. Mr. Bush's whole political life has depended on this, the availability of the corporate standard register and how it centers on image. As a presidential candidate, certainly, he took maximal advantage of this each time an issue-focused and pointedly factual question came his way. Especially so when the question was from a reporter or citizen not quite clued in to the narrowed boundaries of "fairness" in the corporate communicative culture of national politics.

The same in the so-called "debates" with Al Gore. Dubya simply ignored the question; perhaps he didn't follow it. In place of an answer he recited as much of his "message"-relevant autobiography, dropping in as many of the targeted words and expressions as he could in the sincerest first-person. Again and again we heard: that he was Governor of Texas, the second largest state of the Union; someone who got things accomplished by finding compromises with Democrats; someone whose state's schoolchildren had improved reading and math scores; someone whose state was making progress on…; someone who was—by contrast to Clinton—morally clean (or at least repentant); someone who was—by contrast to Gore—modest (or at least quietly smug);…. "Hey, I'm not perfect; but I'm *really trying*!" ("Message?" Gee, because, as he says, he has really been trying in the past, he will really try in the future, lack of apparent fluency and knowledge notwithstanding.)

In at least two of the televised presidential debates, the cocky and confident Al Gore tried time and again to do the same thing to Bush in his out-of-order and rule-breaking direct address. With a display of precisely mobilized detail, he would attempt to expose Dubya's evasions and contradictions, his lack of control of detail, or even comprehension of the previous question—all to no avail. The "message" was that Gore had joined the so-called "liberal press"—you know, the ones who *ask all those trick questions* that try to pry positions on issues out of a candidate, the ones who try to expose the depth with which a candidate knows answers to—can make accurate denotational prose about—issues of fact. (That's just what Dubya couldn't do, of course. But did it matter?) So by sharp contrast to Bush, all fidgeting and little tics and nervous re-posturing aside, Gore conveyed a counterproductive "message" of being one of those folks who don't understand "message," but are focused on issues, issues, issues. Brimming with issues; overflowing with them. Good grief, knowledgeable about them! Allied with that part of the press corps who don't stick to the rules of "message." You know, the ones with perhaps a little whiff of the late Izzy Stone about them? Bush didn't have to answer, of course; all he had to do was make that look into the camera: "Who *is* this guy? Why's he *pestering* me?" (Even mainstream reporters had stopped by this time.)

Given this as our style of political communication, so-called "voter apathy" is better seen as the public's sharp implicit understanding of what their votes have become. They are little more than market acts, buying into a narrow "message" field increasingly divergent from the realm of actual political issues and increasingly irrelevant to where such issues are shaped and decided (could it be big-donor occasions and private briefings for corporate executives?). "Issues," recall, are either "message"-relevant, or to be avoided. For this reason, who among us ever believed that what candidate George W. Bush put forward as his "issues" *were actually his issues*, his or his major backers' real program, and not just "message"-material? In a way, the more convincing he has been via "message," the more he has pressed his issues—which have been the very articulated "issues" everyone thought was just "message!" North Slope oil flowing and old-stand timber falling; regulatory agencies humming business' tunes; the rich paying nothing much in taxes; nuclear sabers rattling and Star Wars missiles at the ready; etc.

But: when you're handed lemons, make lemonade, right? The September 11, 2001 terrorist bombings could not have been better for the actualization of Dubya's "message." Mr. Bush can issue threats, all right; that's a distinct and ever-present aspect of his "message"-identity, the Texas "law-and-order" lawman recruiting the frontier posse—for his Christian *jihad*, a.k.a. "crusade." Remember how the use of that C-word in a not carefully scripted outburst in those angry September days scared the bejeezus out of people in the orbit of Islam? To this—as it was first called—"war," then toned down to "campaign," and now, alas, back to "war," we've all been summoned in the last year. Now it has become a movie with the U.S. Marshals closing in on the armed and dangerous villains holed up—somewhere… perhaps… we think… well, at least there's no evidence to the contrary. The whole administration has been shouting to Mr. Bin Laden and his dastardly minions, "We've got you surrounded!" And the trick will be to keep the audience, the American public, identifying with those grateful townsfolk who appreciate that the Head Marshal is "really trying" to cope with "evil." Everything has got to be aligned with this "message," assimilated to it. One way or another, it will have to be sustained in little ways—Pennsylvania hard-coal miners in summer, 2002—and big ones—Iraq in the pre-election autumn and its triumphant aftermath.

That's My Bush!

So note that Mr. Bush and his entire administration are now dressed in the metaphorical verbal
battle fatigues of the "war on terrorism." And while
in this realm they are "really trying," assimilating all
and sundry to its chain-complex of identifications,
they are really trying to jettison—and have the public
forget—about the vast and contentious domestic
agenda, including doing something about matters economic and corporate. (These have thus far not yielded
such good "message"; hence, they were determinedly
erased in the midterm elections with the cooperation
of Democrats.)

But, in the realms of "message," "war" is war.
After the September attacks, even *The New York Times*
cheered "Mr. Bush's New Gravitas" on 12 October
2001, the day following an East Room press conference. "He seemed more confident, determined, and
sure of his purpose and was in full command of the
complex array of political and military challenges that
he faces," gushed the editorial page: "Mr. Bush clari-
fied and sharpened his positions on several important
issues." Perhaps because the positions the *Times* dis-
cerned happened to be closer to *theirs*!

So they were quick to award Dubya's vocal
performance the Gravvy Award, notwithstanding his
delivery was very much like what they had been exco-
riating him for earlier. There's still a paint-by-word
rhetoric of "message" in the transcript of the
President's answers to questions. Like that thousand

little bursts of light in a network, each word, with its image-enhancing "message"-relevance can be thrown in to connect with the others to paint an image of something—something, but what?—in the area of concern. There's still the sense of a corporate-standard language register that *alludes to* an important policy area one might want to denote, but having alluded to it, moves on to allude to something else, the some-times ungrammatical textual contiguity of them being left for us—if not the *Times*!—still to parse as denota-tional text:

> "I appreciate diplomatic talk. But I'm more inter-ested in action and results. I am absolutely deter-mined, absolutely determined, to <u>rout</u> *terrorism* <u>out</u> where *it* exists and bring *them* to justice. We learned a good lesson on September 11: that there is evil in this world....
> "And it is my duty as the president of the United States to use the resources of this great nation, a freedom-loving nation, a compassionate nation, a nation that understands <u>values</u> of <u>life</u> and <u>rout</u> ter-rorism <u>out</u> where it exists. And we're going to <u>get</u> PLENTY OF NATIONS a <u>chance</u> to do so." [11 October 2001]

Note here the combination of numerous "mes-sage"-words and -expressions, the very stuff of stand-ing tall and silent and tough and ready-for-action in the same first-person casting as was so effective in the 2000 campaign. Note the charming, leftover phrasal ornamentation no doubt still lingering somewhere in memory from the three excellent set speeches that Mr.

Bush had delivered in September, 2001, a couple of weeks before ("this great nation,... of life"). And of course there are the howlers. There are errors of agreement, as in "terrorism...it...them." There are malapropisms, as in "rout out." There are register shifts, as in "plenty of nations." There are substandard locutions, as in "values of life," "get...a chance."

But look at the President's attempt at policy- or issue-talk: it's still as confused as anything the *Times* or Jay Leno was squawking about from the campaign on, until that point. Did he mean "rooting out" terrorists or "routing" them? Is he "giving many nations [where terrorism exists] a chance to root out—or rout—terrorists from their soil" or "getting many nations [together] while this nation has a chance so to do?" What, Mr. President, is the specific policy that follows upon our great, compassionate, freedom-loving understanding of "values [*sic*!] of life?" New gravitas? Gimme a break!

Sure, Mr. *New York Times*-man, the poetry-to-your-ears was that he said big-government (rather than libertarian) things, and internationalist (rather than iso-lationist) things. That's your interpretation, and those are merely implications for your issues. What you're not understanding, however, is that the "message" is still composed out of those fulsome malapropisms and anacolutha and incoherences and agrammatisms because *it's just the use of the "message"-word itself that counts*. It's still poetry of "message." Its coherence with what else is going on, as in the discourse of rationality presumably located elsewhere in the administration (one hopes), seems hardly to be at issue. Time has borne this out. It's unmistakable in Mr. Bush's unscripted, unrehearsed, un-Tel-e-Prompt-R-ed speech.

Language used in the expository mode, used to create argument and therefore, at its most successful, to become the instrument of reason and rationality, is clearly not one of Mr. Bush's attributes. This is not Lincoln. This is not Kennedy. Neither Roosevelt. Whatever else we think of him, not Mr. Clinton. These were Presidents for whom language was both a *renvoi*, a hearkening back, to the experiences of literary imagination made concrete in words, and to systematic use of language for critical thought such as we do in science, in religion for narrative and theological investigation, etc. Whatever the field. Mr. Bush's is a phrasebook notion of political "message"-language, straight out of anxious corporate standard, in which saying the right terms, with luck in a poetically perfect arrangement, is all the message there is.

It's emphatically not just the problem of "soundbites," as print journalists and their partisans in academia keep saying. This is just killing the media messenger. Short excerpts from longer texts can powerfully outline and encapsulate a message while not necessarily being only "message:" "Absolute power corrupts absolutely"; "$E = mc^2$"; "Tune in, turn on, drop out." If you can find an actual *message* to summarize, that is (in the non-insider sense of the term), one otherwise developed with a fluency of overall argument, with all due complexity of exposition that it requires.

Think of the high and low points of the American presidency manifest across the range of its venues for speaking, for using language. Mr. Lincoln's Gettysburg Address (that he wrote himself), in its 272-word final version, is the most concentrated, effective, and sustained union of a rhetorical argument within Baconian—Jeffersonian democracy and an identity-piece—Lincoln's identity—of self-fashioning as humble, plainspoken, King-James-Bible-to-Declaration-of-Independence Eucharistic Americanism. It is one of the best moments in the entire speech-canon of presidents. By comparison, Mr. Bush's speechwriters for his National Cathedral memorial address of 14 September 2001, and his subsequent address to a joint session of Congress of 20 September, also gave him not at all bad examples.

But, linguistically speaking in the politics of recognition, we recognize what Mr. Bush is and what his "message"-folk want him to be by the way he speaks on those relatively unscripted—even if carefully manipulated—occasions. And we must say, that notwithstanding his scripted eloquence on memorial and commemorative days, Dubya's spoken identity ought, perhaps, to give us pause. And that is so particularly in these days of rather knee-jerk "patriotism," in which criticism of the individual who happens to be titular President is easily recast as disloyalty to the country (or so The White House would have it).

In our politics, identity is "message" embodied. So listen to the language. Where, as Julia Ward Howe would have it, Lincoln, verbally embodied, would have Americans die for Freedom, Bush would have us die for Management. I'm not certain we're all, as they say in those parts, "on message." ■

Look for these titles by Prickly Paradigm, and others to come: